1

THE MINISTRY MECHANICS

BUILDING THE CHURCH - EQUIPPING THE LEADER

BY JEREMY JOHNSON & CHRIS HUGHES

Table of Contents

Foreword

The Church is a beautiful gift to us all. It is no mistake that Jesus chose to impact the world through the alternative community that we know as the Church. It is where we get a glimpse of our future... a sneak peek of what will come to pass as Jesus returns and we are ushered into the glorious beauty of our eternal destiny, blessed with the new heavens and new earth.

Sounds pretty amazing, doesn't it?

But let us not forget, the Church lives in the tension of the "already but not yet" ...and this very tension is why the encouragement you find in this book from Jeremy and Chris is so valuable. The Church may give us a glimpse of what is to come, but most days it doesn't look that way. And maybe more importantly, it definitely doesn't feel that way. As ministry leaders we do not only recognize that tension, we live within that tension.

When speaking with new pastors and church planters, I often say that pastoring a church is similar to raising your children in one specific way: it is both incredibly rewarding and incredibly challenging. If you do not have children of your own, you're just going to have to trust me on this. My amazing wife, Monica, and I have been blessed with six children, and just for kicks, we had all six in only six years. I have first hand knowledge of both the rewards and the challenges of parenting. Leading the church which God has entrusted to you is similar. You will encounter days where you feel you are on the mountaintop, celebrating some of the fruits of your labor. Then there are other days where the struggle is real, the trail is steep, you are unsure if you are making a difference, and you wonder if you will ever reach the summit.

As pastors, we benefit from regular reminders and helpful advice to keep us focused no matter which type of day we are experiencing. Throughout their ministries, Jeremy and Chris have experienced their fair share of both sunny mountaintops and dark, steep trails. God has stretched them through these experiences, and what they have learned as a result are the distilled truths they are sharing through this book and through their ministry, The Ministry Mechanics.

There are several things you will notice as you begin to read. First, it literally feels like you are sitting at a coffee-shop and just talking life and ministry with Jeremy and Chris. They are real guys, with genuine in-the-trenches ministry experience. Neither has a pretentious bone in his body. They have no desire to impress people, only a desire to help people. Second, they are incredibly open about their lives and church experiences. Oftentimes ministry books feel like highlight reels, jumping from one success to the next. Yet we do not only learn from what goes well, but also from what doesn't go as planned. Jeremy and Chris allow us to learn from the totality of their ministry service. Third, they focus on the practical rather than the theoretical. Again, this book arose from their life as pastors and from their ongoing coaching work with churches across the country. They discuss foundational issues, such as questions related to one's calling, and they dig into the nuts-and-bolts of a variety of topics we all face as pastors, from evaluating ministry programs to caring for your people to navigating change. Finally, this book is filled with hope. Jesus is our hope, and Jesus at work through local churches is the hope our world desperately needs. Jeremy and Chris are on this journey with us, encouraging pastors, reminding us of our calling, inspiring us to be prayerful, thoughtful and intentional in how we approach this beautiful gift, Christ's Church.

Seek God: may He speak to you through the pages of this book.
Trust God: may He guide you into taking action.
Love God: may you give God your best as His love flows into you
and through you to the people He has brought into your life and
the ministry to which He has called you.

grace+peace,

Jason Daye
Vice-president of Ministry Mobilization, Outreach Inc
Colorado Springs, Colorado

Intro

Let's go ahead and get this out of the way early...we don't fix cars. Heck, we don't even really know anything about cars. We'll help you work on yours, but we can assure you that you won't be happy with the results. Chris owns a 1969 Ford Fairlane and Jeremy's grandfather had a 1967 Mustang, but that's about our only claims to fame when it comes to automobiles. That being said, cars and churches have a lot in common. They both have complex designs. They're powerful (sometimes). They get you from where you are to where you want to be. Cars use fuel and oxygen to create a spark and produce momentum. The church uses God's Word and the Holy Spirit to light a spark and give every person that has an encounter with God a new direction. From time to time cars, Christians, and churches need tune-ups.

That's why we do what we do. We want to get our hands dirty and get into the nuts and bolts of growth and depth and health. We want to get under the hood, bust some knuckles, and work together to change the perception AND reality for leaders and churches all over the world.

There are tons of great books on ministry out there but this one is different because it's our story and it's how our story intersects with your story. We aren't a program. We aren't a 40 days of anything. We aren't a one-size-fits-all strategy. We aren't theologians and don't even pretend to play one on TV. We are just two normal guys who have been blessed by some unique experiences in life and ministry. Of course you'll find practical advice on leadership and ministry in these pages, but that all flows out of our testimony. It's no accident that you are reading this book. We want you to stay with it and allow God to work in your heart as you turn each page. We want you to be greatly inspired to push yourself to grow and reach your God-given potential.

God completely changed our lives because of the local church and local pastors. We firmly believe that it's the hope of the world. That being said, we want to help people follow Jesus, we want to help churches reach their full potential, and we want help pastors know they aren't alone on this journey. Get ready for some real talk, some transparent and open conversation about life, ministry, and the church…not cars.

Chris & Jeremy

CHRIS'S STORY

CHAPTER 1

THE MINISTRY MECHANICS

I (Chris) come from a long line of storytellers. My grandparents and uncles had an amazing gift of bringing stories to life. Getting ready for bed or out on a camping trip meant that there was a good story on the way. Some were scary. Some were funny. Some were historic. And some were pure fantasy. I've always loved good stories and storytellers. I'm drawn to the details and characters and emotion. I've lost count at the number of times I've told my story. God has used my personal story to impact thousands of people all over the United States. It's not that it's that incredible or unbelievable. It's that my story is...my story. I know it better than anyone else. It's intensely personal and can instantly transport me back to the moments and memories from the past.

I didn't grow up in a particularly religious home. We were pretty connected to an old-school Baptist church when I was really little because my great grandparents were really committed to an old-school baptist church. Because it was important to them, it was important to us. Older family members have a way of keeping a family connected and growing. Regular church attendance ended for us on a Wednesday night, shortly after my Great Grandfather passed away. I'll never forget it. We got ready and drove to the church out in the country. We got out of the car and walked up to the doors. We weren't dressed extremely casually, but I do remember that my mom was wearing khaki pants. As we climbed the stairs to enter the church, we were met at the door by some "enforcers" of the rules. They let my mom know that we wouldn't be allowed in because she was wearing pants. At that time and at that place, it was viewed as inappropriate for a woman to wear pants to church. We turned around, got back in the car and rarely went to church together as a family ever again.

We sort of became Christmas or Easter (*or not and!*) people at that point. Once a year, we'd give it the old college try and show up at a different country church with a different country preacher with the same things we had experienced before. The red carpet, the musty building, the lady playing the organ who seemed extremely close to dying, the Sunday School attendance sign, the hymnals and the old man in our pew who slept through most of the service. Once the service was over, it was like we had checked a box and done our duty for the year. It had officially become a tradition rather than a spiritual encounter with a living God.

Over time, our commitment to this routine faded. We would make the occasional token effort, but it wasn't anything real. Then Christmas of 1995 happened. I was invited by a friend from my high school to attend a Christmas program at a local United Methodist Church in a ridiculously small town. This town had an IGA Supermarket, an elementary school, a bank and 50+ churches. I thought this would be another run-of-the-mill church experience, but I was wrong. A young pastor walked in and made a bee-line for me, expressed genuine interest in me and seemed legitimately glad that I was there. I made it through the program but I made the mistake of filling out the card! Back in those days, if you filled out the card, you had a pastor visit your home within 16 minutes of the service ending! When he pulled in the driveway, my mom immediately asked me to cut him off at the pass. We didn't like "drop by" visits from anyone!

I went out to the driveway and chatted it up with Joe Manis, the pastor of the church. He was so different from any of the other guys that I had met. He sounded like me. He joked like me. I liked him. Joe went on to tell me about a youth group swimming event that was coming up at a local college. I asked if there would be girls there. He confirmed that there would be girls there and I accepted the invite! I showed up and awkwardly found my seat in the church van and off we went to this thing that I knew nothing about. As we pulled onto the campus, there were college students everywhere that were friendly and welcoming. This was significant for a kid like me. I wasn't a cool kid and I wasn't a particularly smart kid. I never really fit in at any table in our high school lunchroom, so I was starving for a connection. These students and this pastor genuinely seemed to like me for me.

After we swam, played some kickball and got cleaned up, we went into a huge auditorium with a big stage. There were tons of instruments up there. Guitars, drums, bass guitar, keys and amplifiers for them all. This was new for me. These were things that I actually cared about. I was a musician and loved any music of any kind. The countdown ended and they struck the first chord. I couldn't believe it. The music was amazing. So different from anything I'd ever experienced at a church gathering. I could sense something stirring in my heart, but I didn't even know what to do with that feeling. I just knew I found something that I really liked. So… I kept going back.

On a cold weekend in January of 1996, I gave my heart to Jesus at Resurrection, a Methodist youth camp, in Gatlinburg, TN. Pastor Joe gave me a study Bible and wrote a personal inscription that meant so much to me. This sparked something incredible in my heart. I found a place to belong and a purpose to commit my life to. I tore through the pages of that Bible and read it cover-to-cover 3 times in the first year.

Joe and I kept meeting regularly to discuss what was happening inside of my heart and mind. He gently coached me through what it meant to make Jesus the Lord of my life. Joe taught me to study the Bible, gave me chances to serve, and fanned a flame in my heart that is still burning today. Joe asked me to share from my heart at our student gatherings. Joe asked me to give the lesson during a Sunday morning youth service. Joe asked me to mow the grass on Easter weekend. He saw how hungry I was to go deeper and he helped me redirect my energy into building a story for God instead of a story without God.

As the weeks went on, I started to feel another change coming. Was there more to life than chasing girls and playing sports? While changing this part of my journey wasn't easy, it was clear that God was moving again. All I wanted to do was earn a college scholarship to play any kind of sport possible. I knew I wasn't going to set the world on fire because of my intellect, but sports seemed to be a possibility. After breaking my hand on the first day of freshman football and getting destroyed on a big hit on my first day back at football practice, it was quickly becoming clear that football might not be the best plan of action. So, I joined the golf team. Nothing screams cool like joining the golf team. I was finding some success as a golfer and eventually got a few offers from smaller schools to play golf. It was a dream come true. I signed to play at Milligan College in Johnson City, Tennessee. Everything was falling into place. During my senior year of high school, I found my groove. Scholarship locked down, a new sense of direction, and loving Jesus. Life was good. How could it get better? I met a girl and it did.

I really struggled with dating relationships. I didn't have a great grasp of what a healthy and Godly dating relationship was supposed to look like. While most things in my life changed easily when I became a Christ-follower, relationships took the most time to change. Before I really met Jesus, I got an invitation to a leadership conference at the University of Tennessee at Chattanooga and met a girl from a place near my hometown. In a word: Hot. She was beautiful. She was an incredibly talented dancer. She was Tennessee's Junior Miss. This girl was a catch.

As my Junior prom drew close, I realized that every girl in my high school was either mad at me or had no idea who I was. So, I thought I'd take a shot and ask the girl I met in Chattanooga. To my amazement, she remembered me and even said yes! Prom date with an amazing girl in a word: Disaster. I blew it. I was terrible company and it did not go well. I thought I'd never hear from or see this girl again. But, as time went on and after I came to know Jesus, I got up the nerve to ask for forgiveness and begged her to go out with me again. To my surprise, she said yes again. Now that I was walking with Jesus, it was time to go about things differently. I wanted to do everything I could to make sure I didn't make the same mistakes again. So, I did what every good 90's Christian did: we went to a Jars Of Clay/Third Day/Michael W. Smith concert. This was a double date with another amazing couple from her hometown. We hung out, laughed, and everyone really enjoyed their evening.

After the night was over, we started the drive back to her house down Interstate 75. The conversation was so different this time around. It was natural and pleasant. While we were rolling down the highway, she asked me why things were so different in my life. I was able to share the story of my encounter with Jesus in depth. I sensed something big was happening and really dialed into the story and the details. I was driving dangerously slow on the interstate because I was so into the story. Kelly was blown away that my walk with God had changed my life in that big of a way. I asked her if she wanted that too, and she said yes. So, on the side of the interstate, I led Kelly to the Lord. This was the first time I had ever shared my faith with anyone. It was an amazing moment. We finished the drive home, I kissed her good night, and was so excited about what God was doing in my life.

After a few more dates, our relationship was really growing. It was the first time to have my faith really be at the center of my relationship with a girlfriend in a healthy way. We were definitely growing close. Talking on the phone as often as possible (or as much long distance calling as my parents would pay for). I got to see her perform a few times for various events. I even bought her a study Bible so we could grow together and talk about what God was doing in our lives. Then, one Sunday afternoon, I got a phone call. It was from Kelly's mom, Janice. She was calling with the saddest news I'd ever received. She shared with me that Kelly had been killed in a car accident on the way to dance practice that morning. My heart sank. I was so incredibly sad. Things changed quickly when she shared with me that Kelly had mentioned our conversation in the car on the side of the interstate. She was so thankful for Kelly's decision and asked if I would be willing to share it at her funeral and sing a song. I was so honored that she asked me and quickly said yes. While I was heartbroken, I knew that God was going to use her story in a mighty way.

That night at the funeral was overwhelming. So many teens and parents alike were in the building from all over her community. It was an incredible response and spoke to her character. She was loved by everyone. The pastor at the church that hosted her funeral couldn't have been more gracious. He could sense my anxiousness and worked to calm me and walked me through what to say. I shared and sang and it was over in a flash. I poured my heart out to everyone in that room, along with some other speakers and her dad. This wasn't a funeral, it was a church service. It was a Holy Spirit moment. You could sense the power of God in a big way. During the invitation, more than one hundred people, mostly students, gave their life to Christ that night. That sight gave purpose to the pain I was feeling. God cemented in my heart a passion to reach the lost with the Gospel and share the story of my changed life with as many people as possible. I recently connected with Kelly's mom on social media and she shared with me the power of that moment and let me know that she still uses Kelly's Bible for her devotion. Wow, just wow.

I was in love with Jesus before this tragic event, but now I was white hot on fire for the Lord. I spoke with as many church youth groups as I possibly could, sang at every church in our area, and did everything within my power to serve God in every way possible. God was developing a call on my life to serve Him in ministry. I was asked to volunteer with a friend at a local church as a student ministry leader. My new pastor, Rick Harrell, was such an incredible encouragement to me. He was a Godly man and a great example to me of what it looks like to be a Godly husband and father. He also walked me through what it meant to follow God's call on your life. It was such a God send.

After graduating high school, I was ready to go play golf in college. I was excited about the next chapter. During that summer, a close friend asked me to go visit a church with her in Birmingham, Alabama over a weekend. This church had actually called me and offered me a "student ministry internship" at their church. I didn't even know what in the world that meant and politely declined. However, since my friend was going to visit the church, I decided to give it a visit and see what it was all about. I was blown away. Until this point, the only church experience I'd ever known was banjos and blue haired ladies who were just loitering in Heaven's waiting room. This church was alive. It had amazing music, powerful teaching, a vibrant student ministry, and was reaching people in their community.

After one weekend, I asked if I could stay for the rest of the summer and they said yes. I drove back home, packed my stuff, and got back down to Birmingham as soon as I could. I loved it. It was exactly the thing God had for me. After the summer, things had gone well. I was getting ready to go to Milligan College and start my golf career. That was until Steve Wright, the student pastor, asked me to stay on as a paid intern. They offered to help with some schooling and pay me some money. I couldn't believe it. I called my golf coach and told my parents that I wouldn't be attending Milligan College and I wouldn't be playing golf. I had found the very thing that God had called me to do. That was in the summer of 1997. I've been a part of planting five churches and seen hundreds come to know Jesus. I'm married to the love of my life, Emily, and we have two amazing kids. And now I'm shifting my focus from a single church to "The Church." God took a young man with no perspective or experience and bowled me over with His faithfulness.

There are many more details and years to my story, but all these years later, the center is still the same: God is blowing my mind with the way He is moving in my ministry. I'm so in love with serving Jesus. I'm more passionate today than I've ever been about seeing lives changed forever by Jesus. The Ministry Mechanics are poised to reach a brand new audience and expand our calling. I believe that we're going to be a part of helping people, pastors, and leaders find their calling. I believe that we're going to help churches and businesses grow like never before. Our brightest days are still in front of us. We're just getting started.

Jeremy's Story

Chapter 2

The Ministry Mechanics

Since I (Jeremy) was a young child, the local church has played an integral role in my life. I joke often that I was seemingly born in a church. I don't know this for sure but I think I was born in a Sunday school room of the church that I grew up in. Of course everyone tells me that I was actually born in a hospital. I do know without a doubt I was there within just a few days of my birth and I haven't strayed too far ever since. I suppose I have my mom to thank for that.

I grew up in a half-Christian home. You may or may not be able to relate. My mom was a faithful believer and she took me to church every Sunday morning, Sunday night, Wednesday night and sometimes in between. It would seem that we had a key to the church with all of the frequent trips to the corner of Main and Willow streets. It may also seem that way because my papaw owned the neighborhood gas station right next door. I didn't really mind the constant trips to church, for some reason I thought it was fun and I developed an early appreciation and genuine love for the church and for ministry.

My dad was disinterested in attending church throughout my childhood. He liked to sleep in on Sundays and never seem to fit in at the church we were attending. My extended family was very involved in the church, especially in the area of music and worship. I began to develop a passion for music as well. In fact when I was just a couple of years old, I would go in the choir with my mom and I would turn around and direct the choir. I suppose you could say that I had the desire to be a leader at a very young age.

Around the same age, I would go visit my uncle and aunt in their home and I would stand behind a ceramic owl in their living room and I would pretend to preach. The owl was my pulpit. I could barely string together sentences but I was on fire to preach the Word even if it was gibberish. I was modeling what I had seen since I was at the church so much. I knew early on what it looked like to be a pastor and a leader.

I had a pastor who modeled how to be a leader extremely well, his name was John Andrus. He was the pastor at my church for 31 years before he decided to retire after a very successful tenure. He was the consummate shepherd of people and loved others like I had never seen before and have rarely seen since. Our pastor was a part of our family and I'm not only thankful for his influence in my walk with Christ but also the impact he had on my leadership style of loving people. He was the first one to teach me what it meant to not just pastor a church, but how to pastor people and treat them the right way.

When I was nine years old, I was at a revival with my family and accepted Christ in my life. Even though I was so young, I committed my life to God. At that tender young age I really didn't know what that meant, but I was willing to seek after Him with everything within me.

Fast forward seven years later, I was in high school and I was very active in church. I sang on Sundays quite often and had an active role in the youth group. By this time, I was being asked to sing in different churches around the area. One of those churches was right near my home in Chattanooga, TN. I remember it was a Wednesday night and many of my friends from high school were there. As I began to sing during the invitation time, I remember the overwhelming movement of the Holy Spirit. That was the very moment that I felt God's calling on my life to dedicate the rest of my days on this Earth to serve Him.

That was the moment that I was called into a lifetime of ministry. Over 20 years later, I remember that moment like it was yesterday. In fact when I start to have doubt, I am reminded that I was called into ministry for a purpose. I think about how real that moment was and immediately my mind and heart are flooded with my original calling. If God called me to ministry, He would never abandon me through the hard seasons of life. Trust me if you are called by God there will be difficult seasons. The best leaders know how to push through and stay faithful.

Following my call into ministry, I began to dive right in the deep end. I began my own Evangelistic ministry. I know it sounds crazy and a bit on the ambitious side, but even though I didn't know anything yet, I felt God had given me a gift to share with others. So I began leading worship and speaking at churches across the southeast. I hit the road and ministered in youth revivals, retreats and camps. I was building relationships with so many people and in turn it created a network of people who I have now known for a couple of decades. One thing I learned is that you can't do ministry without people. This is something we will explore in detail in a later chapter.

Not only was I building relationships, I was gaining much needed experience. Sometimes we dream and plan and study for many years without taking the natural step to just do ministry. When we get to the point where we think we have it all figured out, things change and then we have to dream, plan and study some more. It's a constant cycle that never seems to end. Sometimes you just have to go out and do it. Through that process of repetition, you will learn, you will fail and you will discover how to do ministry and maybe more importantly you discover what not to do. That's ok, that is how we grow and how we refine the calling God gives us. As I was continuing my journey into ministry, I felt my next natural step was college. I figured that's what everyone else was doing, so I did the same. I had what seemed like a cup of coffee at a small liberal arts university in East Tennessee but found out quickly that place just wasn't my speed. I took some time off and then I finally landed at Trevecca Nazarene University in the heart of Nashville, TN. It was there I made so many friends and met the person that I would eventually marry. Throughout that experience I learned so much about life. What I didn't learn about in my college classes was the practical side of ministry, which I still find true in most higher education institutions today. The theology training is superb in most places, however the practical application of how to be a pastor is somewhat obsolete. I am hopeful that one of the things we do is to shed some light on how to lead in a practical way and close the gap from the university level.

A few years after my entrance into Trevecca, I got married and began my first full time church position as a Student/College Pastor in Georgia. I experienced many firsts that year, including how to be a husband and how to lead a student ministry. I was learning what it meant to be a pastor for the very first time. The next year, I learned that I was going to be a father. It was all a tough balance that I am sure many struggle with. It was an overwhelming transition that first year. The student ministry was seeing tremendous growth. My first Wednesday night on staff, we had 12 students. I thought to myself, this is going to be quite a task to see growth. The morale was low, apathy had set in because they had seen three student pastors in the previous four years. The culture was unhealthy and I knew it would be difficult but really the only direction was up for this group. It couldn't sink any lower than it was at that point.

God began to take over and we started to see exponential growth. I was investing in those students like they had never seen before and many were surrendering their lives to Christ. Within a year, those 12 students had multiplied to 75-85 students consistently. Many of those students today are mothers and fathers. They are doctors, actors, musicians and teachers. I am very proud of the work that was accomplished during that season and the people I was blessed to help develop throughout my tenure in Georgia.

After about 2 years at the church, my daughter Jada was born nine weeks early. She had a birth defect that caused her to have surgery right after birth and she was in the hospital for seven weeks. While she was in the hospital, I was notified by the pastor of the church that my position was being eliminated and I was being let go without cause or warning. The church wanted to build a daycare center and needed my salary to pay the daycare director. It made no sense at the time, the student ministry was growing leaps and bounds and we were seeing God change students forever.

As a green rookie in ministry, I couldn't understand how a church could do that. Well, it was actually the pastor and I learned quickly that the church is just a place made up of flawed people, not much different than the world. Even though that wasn't God's desire in the beginning, it is now filled with humans who sometimes do things that do not reflect the bride of Christ. It was a painful first lesson in the reality of the church and a harsh way to discover the importance of people in your life, the right ones and the wrong ones.

Following this ordeal, I would hit the road again with my own evangelistic ministry. This time for several years. God used me in different ways to build up the church. In a way it was very appealing to me, I could go into a church, make an impact and then leave. I wasn't exposed to their problems or the fundamental issues that they may have. Even if people didn't like me, it was ok, I would never hear about it. In a way I was insulated and isolated in this role of guest worship leader and speaker.

Throughout my life on the road, my marriage became more difficult. By this time we had our second child, this time a boy, who we named Skyler. It was a juggling act to raise two young children, to be a good husband and to keep an evangelistic ministry going. I began to get road weary and I knew that God was making a change in my life. I got on my knees and began to ask God what was next in my life. I fasted for 21 days believing that God had an answer for me. At the end of the 21 days, the vision was clear. God was calling me back to full time church staff ministry. He was beginning to lay the groundwork and the heart to plant a church.

In 2008, we moved from Tennessee to Orlando to begin a new life. I went on staff as an associate pastor at a growing church in central Florida. During my time there, the economy went into the tank and the church was having major financial problems. By the end of my second year, I knew that God was telling me to make the tough decision to plant a church twelve miles away in a thriving community. Sometimes if you are unwilling to move, God simply throws you out of the plane and watches you fly on your own. This was one of those opportunities to fly. The church staff was nearly liquidated and I was the last pastor to go. My salary had been cut 30% and I knew it wouldn't be long after the salary cuts. They released me on a Wednesday, ten days later our church plant was meeting for the first time in a house.

We began Element Church with humble beginnings, six adults and six kids in a living room. Every week we were adding families and pretty soon the living room was past capacity. We even built a kids ministry area in our garage. After a couple of months in our house, we branched out to the YMCA. For the next year we built our core group and started to see an impact on the community. We had an event before launch on Good Friday night that drew over 1200 people. We began to grow and see exponential growth during the first two years. It was legitimately the greatest season of ministry in my life. Then something happened that would rock my world and change my life forever.

On a normal Wednesday morning one December, my day started like it had for many years. I woke up and immediately got ready for my busy day as a pastor. Little did I know that I would experience a day that would change the trajectory of my life forever. A day that I will never forget.

If you have gone through difficult situations or tragedies, most of the time you never see them coming, you are blindsided. This held true on this particular day. After my normal morning routine, my wife approached me and asked me to come downstairs into our living room. I could immediately sense that something was wrong. I felt that something was about to drastically change.

I walked down the two flights of stairs into the living room and at that point my front door opened. It was my mentor and friend Tim. I wasn't expecting him on that morning but he said he wanted to be there for support. I sat down on the love seat in my living room and my wife began to cry. She told me that she was leaving and taking the kids to her parents in Missouri. There wasn't a moral failure and there wasn't any issue that couldn't have been worked out. It was the end of the line for her and I had to accept it. As you could imagine, I was completely shocked, saddened and just devastated. I never thought in a million years that God would allow this to happen. Divorce wasn't in my vocabulary. My parents never got a divorce and both sets of my grandparents were married for 55 plus years. This was a foreign concept to me. I now was forced to come to the realization that this was a possibility.

On that day, I stood on my front porch and watched my wife and kids drive away. I waved at them as they pulled off, not knowing if we would ever be together as a family again. As I turned to walk back into an empty home in Orlando, my heart felt even more empty. Just the day before the same home was filled with laughter and my two were kids running through the house. My house was normally buzzing with activity but on this day, it was dark, lonely and silent.

I was a husband, father, successful church planter and lead pastor of this awesome church that I loved. In a split second, all of that was in jeopardy. My existence was completely shattered, I was certainly a broken man and I was overtaken with the sound of deafening silence. In those crucial early moments I had a very important decision to make. Do I wallow in my sorrow, do I give up and get out of ministry, never to set foot back into a church? Do I get angry with the God that allows this to happen? Trust me, it certainly crossed my mind, but that would have been foolish.

My other option was to scrape myself off of the floor and carry on the calling and purpose that God had placed in my heart. I could choose to just go through this season or I could choose to grow through this season. I was at a crucial crossroads in my life and I thankfully chose to grow through my season. I wanted to allow God to change me and change my heart through the process of pain and hurt. I had to come to the understanding that God uses every drop of pain for purpose. We may not see it when we are in the middle of the storm, but I now see it years removed from that dark season.

In the days and weeks following my wife's departure, God began to do a work in me that can't be explained. I knew that whether or not God healed my marriage really didn't change the fact that He wanted to heal my heart and my brokenness. He was more concerned about what was happening inside of me than what was happening around me. I started the process with an empty tank but little by little God began to refill my soul again. That's the kind of God He is, a God that replenishes when you feel that you can't go on. He provides strength and courage, even when you feel you've lost everything.

Just a short few months after that infamous Wednesday, my wife decided to make it final and file for divorce. During those three months, I fought for my marriage and did everything in my power to save it. I went to counseling and tried to get her to go with me but God didn't allow that to happen. I tried to save it even after the divorce was final that summer but to no avail. It was over and I had to move forward with my life. There was a mountain in front of me that I had no clue how to climb and I knew I couldn't do this alone. So I needed to rely on family and friends during this season. I called on over 80 people to be on my prayer team. These were warriors that I knew I could lean on in the face of the battle. They helped me navigate through the difficult waters and the healing process of a divorce after 13 years. My heart needed to be restored back to health, ministry aside. I realized the need for a support system to pray for me and to keep me encouraged to keep fighting.

I will admit there were times of depression and times that I felt lost. I didn't know what God wanted me to do with the rest of my life. I wasn't sure if God could even use me again. I wasn't sure if He wanted to use a divorced guy in ministry. I was then pointed to a passage in Romans that struck a chord with me. It says, "For the gifts and calling of God are irrevocable." Which meant to me that my original calling hadn't changed and the gifts that God had instilled in my life were still intact and were not going away. I wasn't worthless to God, He still wanted to use a broken vessel to be a conduit for His message.

On the day I received the divorce papers, I was desperate and still believing in a miracle. I sent a message through Twitter to my friend Chris Hughes, He sent this word of encouragement back to me that meant so much at the time and even still today. I will never forget his simple yet comforting words:

"So sorry man. How can I help? I'm praying with you! I'm here for you man"

Chris would go on to tell me maybe the greatest words of encouragement that I heard during my darkest hour. He said, "Jeremy I believe that God is going to use you to impact the Kingdom in greater ways than ever before. Your greatest days of ministry are ahead of you, rather than behind you." I really struggled to believe that when he said it because rarely can you see the truth when you are in the
vortex of the struggle. However, that was the spark that I needed to believe that God still had a plan and purpose for me and that my calling wasn't dead.

I wish I could end this chapter by telling you that my marriage was miraculously restored and that my family was put back together. However, that's not my story. While I may never understand why it didn't happen that way, it doesn't change the fact that I trust the one who allowed it. Sometimes the answer that we receive from God isn't the one we want, but He still finds purpose in each answer. He somehow finds a way to take what the enemy meant for evil and transform it in to something good for each of us. I can't tell you that he rescued my marriage, but in the process He rescued me. Today I know that I am a better man after the storm than I ever was before it.

And Chris was right. My greatest days of ministry were ahead of me, not behind me!

STRONGER TOGETHER

CHAPTER 3

THE MINISTRY MECHANICS

Have you ever thought about how God chose to place each planet in order? Positioning them precisely where He wanted them for a special purpose. Not only are they positioned perfectly in order, they all have different functions, sizes and environments that make them unique. Alone in space they are special but when connected they are a masterpiece from God that make up our solar system. Even though each planet has its own unique purpose, each night from our vantage point, the solar system seems to all fit together with perfection. Each planet and star is bright in its own way but when they are combined with others, that's when something really special happens. If you have ever been out in the country at night and looked into the sky, you know how extraordinary an artist God really is. This book has nothing to do with astrology but simply reminds us about the sovereign power and will of God.

God also does that very thing with people by connecting us together for a special purpose. When He puts us in perfect alignment with His will, we begin to see blessings that we could never imagine previously in our life. He creates each of us with a unique purpose and has a unique plan for every single one of our lives. Sometimes it takes a while for each of us to discover that purpose, but when we do, it just all makes sense. It doesn't always happen the way you draw it up on your dream board, but when it happens it feels like it's supposed to be that way. When this takes place, our purpose is magnified and you find the sweet spot of your calling and your life. God doesn't always put the people you want in your life, but He does put the people you need exactly where they're supposed to be.

I (Jeremy) knew I had my own unique purpose and that purpose alone could've had a tremendous impact on the Kingdom. But what would happen if I hadn't realized that ministry wasn't meant to be done alone? Some people are just meant to be in your life and at times it transitions your purpose to something even greater if you are obedient and humble enough to be open to His calling.

I didn't know what I didn't know. Many of us don't until we experience life and God allows us to go through situations to teach us. Through these lessons, He solidifies who we are and who He wants us to be. I didn't realize that my gifts combined with someone else's gifts could be stronger than just mine alone. I didn't know that I needed someone in my life to challenge me and join in this journey to maximize the potential impact in ministry. I heard the scripture about iron sharpening iron and had quoted it quite often. However I didn't really know what that meant just yet. I have always loved collaborating with others and had been a team guy, but I needed a ministry partnership that was completely natural and someone that I clicked with creatively and personality-wise.

I was busy planting a church in Orlando and I really wanted to talk to someone that I knew of as a church planting guru. I wanted to learn everything I could about this crazy world. I had been researching and learning for years but I wanted to learn all the tricks of the trade from someone who I admired as a foremost expert in that field. I was a young Luke Skywalker looking for my Yoda. I was connected on social media with a church planting Yoda-type named Mac, who I had seen around at conferences, but I had never reached out to. At this point like many of our "friends" we were just virtual acquaintances, but had never met. I found out that he was going to be in town and I finally contacted him to see if he would possibly agree to meet for coffee. He sent back a quick response and agreed to meet with me. We had a great meeting at Starbucks and we began to connect further after that initial meeting.

I thought the reason that I met Mac was to tap into his massive knowledge of church planting and his experience of building networks and communities. Although I learned from Mac, there was a greater purpose for connecting with him. There are times when people come into your life for different reasons than you originally imagined. At that point I didn't know what the reason was, I just knew I had to be obedient and that's usually when God shifts gears and the spider web is weaved a little wider. Mac was the flow through to connect me with a complete stranger and a guy that was on a similar path. Little did we know that we needed each other to partner with an identical God-sized vision to pour into leaders and churches.

The very next time that I heard from Mac, he sent me a message and connected me with a guy named Chris Hughes. I didn't know him from Adam, but Mac thought it would be great to connect with him because we were both from East Tennessee. He thought we would hit it off, but I am sure he didn't know exactly how well. Chris was considering planting a church in the Orlando area and I was already on the ground in Orlando doing it. I'm all for networking and this networking connection ended up being the most significant in my ministry.

Chris and I chatted through Twitter messages for a while before we actually met. He would give me feedback on the church's website and was another set of eyes to a guy who had spent hours pouring into the details of a church plant. We found out pretty quickly that we are both perfectionists when it comes to excellence and we visualize things in similar ways. Mac was right; we did have a lot in common, more than he or we both ever realized. Maybe the biggest thing we had in common was the fact that we were both die hard fans of the Tennessee Volunteers. (If you are a fan of the Gators, Crimson Tide, Georgia Bulldogs or any other college football team, please keep reading. God loves you too).

A few months later, Chris told me that he was making the trip to Orlando for the Exponential Conference. Exponential was and still is the biggest church planting conference in the country. He sent me a message and asked if I wanted to meet for a late dinner after the conference. We met at the Mall of Millenia in Orlando and had a great dinner and really connected. We talked about our kids and people we might mutually know in the small world of East Tennessee. It was almost as if we were instantly family. We had a similar style of ministry, a similar vision for the church and we found out very quickly a similar sense of humor, which is always important and sometimes dangerous, in a good way of course.

I remember thinking after that initial meeting, "Man, it would be so cool to work together in ministry, at least in some capacity." After that dinner, we went back to connecting on social media and just being Facebook friends. We would send messages every now and then but at this point he was a church planting guy that I knew. Time went by and a few months later he and his family packed up and moved to North Carolina to lead a church.

Ironically at that same point, my world utterly collapsed. As I wrote in a previous chapter, in those crucial moments I reached out to Chris. What I didn't tell you was the part that I barely knew Chris. We connected a few times when he was in town, but we were not best friends…..yet. I really feel it was orchestrated by the Holy Spirit, almost as if God was saying that He was the guy I needed to reach out to in my darkest moment. Once again despite our vantage point of limited visibility of the future, God was aligning things in our favor. Even though we don't have a clue why, many times in our life God gives us direction that leads us to the very place He desires for us and to the people He desires for us to live in community with. God was closer than a brother during that time of my life, but He also knew that I needed a brother on this earth.

From that moment on, Chris and I communicated often and he was the CEO, chief encouragement officer in my life, which was exactly what I needed as I was going through the most difficult year of my life. Everyone needs a CEO in their life. Something that the ministry world really lacks these days is encouragement. Not just a pat on the back, but honest and positive reinforcement instilled in someone else. This is overlooked and much needed in every leader's heart. When I needed something, Chris and his wife Emily were there and we really solidified our friendship during that season. God was certainly at work, but we still didn't know exactly what He had in store. Our only goal was to be faithful and obedient and let God fill in the details.

During that same summer, Chris sent me a message and asked if I would be willing to come and speak at their church's volunteer training day called "Next Level." At first I didn't know what to think about it; I had mixed emotions. On one hand, I felt that I had nothing to offer the people at his church. Even though I replayed Chris' words of affirmation and encouragement, telling me that God is not done with me and my greatest days of ministry are ahead. It is so difficult to believe that when you are in the middle of it. I still felt the enemy's attack on my life and I didn't feel worthy of such an opportunity.

Then God woke me up from my slumber and called me worthy. I was humbled by just a chance to do ministry again, even if it was just to speak for 45 minutes. It was a light at the end of the tunnel, my redemption coming full circle. It was God's way of saying, "Keep fighting. You are not destroyed and you will have new life in Me." When Chris asked me, I was literally in tears and the peace of God was overwhelming. He offered me $250 and to me at that time that amount of money felt like a million dollars. Of course I would've done it for free. Once again God was providing an opportunity and allowing me to invest in people's lives.

That summer at the event, I stood in a packed room and tried with everything in me to keep it together and play it cool. I over-prepared for that day and had 30 pages of notes. When I opened my mouth to speak in that room, the presence of God was overwhelming. I had a feeling I had never felt before while speaking. I was training the first impressions team, giving them some tips on how to make people feel like a VIP in their church. It certainly wasn't a theological masterpiece, but it didn't need to be. I honestly don't remember anything I said on that day, I just remember how it felt. While I was speaking, the Spirit affirmed my calling. I remember I felt God saying, "This is what you are wired to do. I created you to pour into people and invest in THE Church."

The Mechanics Are Born

One year later, Chris asked me to come on staff at his church in North Carolina part time. For a few months I commuted from Tennessee to North Carolina to help the church grow in any way I could. It was another step in my journey. This was the first time I was hired in a pastoral role following my divorce. I wasn't sure if I would ever serve in a church ever again and then it became a reality. Even though I knew it was part-time and temporary, it was a tremendous opportunity. Once again I was indebted to Chris for believing in me and believing that God could still use me in even greater ways than ever before.

While on staff, Chris and I continued to build our friendship and we began to discover the ministry chemistry that we could have. A couple of months into my time there, we took a trip that would forever change our lives and ministries. On a Sunday after church, we loaded up a truck and a small trailer and made the drive from Franklin, North Carolina to Detroit, Michigan. We went there to help a church plant prepare for their official launch.

When we arrived at the church, it was a 100-plus year old building that was in dire need of some tender, loving care. Our goal was to transform their worship area into a modern worship space as well as give them a quality children's area. With limited resources and a tight schedule, it would have to be an Extreme Makeover, Church Edition venture. We wanted to modernize each space and provide a welcoming environment for people to gather and hear about Jesus.

The transformation that took place over just a couple of days was mind-boggling. We were able to frugally reimagine a space and have this church ready for launch. It's amazing what you can do with a some pipe and drape, paint and plywood. Their children's area went from a blank basement to a colorful, vibrant and most importantly, welcoming venue for kids' ministry.

When we unveiled both areas for the pastor and his wife, they were overwhelmed with the difference. Tears of joy and gratitude filled their eyes and heart. They couldn't understand why a group of guys from North Carolina would care enough to give their time, resources and energy to a group of people that they didn't even know. I will never forget those moments in Michigan, the hugs that we received and the overwhelming outpouring of gratitude. We allowed this pastoral team in Michigan to visualize the possible even when it felt and seemed impossible.

As we got back in the truck, we couldn't stop talking about how much fun we had helping that church. We were buzzing the whole way home with ideas galore. At one point, we talked about how it would be great if we could help more than just that one church. What would it look like if we could help multiple churches? What would it take to help churches and leaders all across the country or even globally? At this point it was just two guys talking about how to best serve the Kingdom of God, because that is what it's all about: Building the Kingdom!

Even though we helped this particular church with aesthetic and physical needs, that isn't really our primary passion and wheelhouse. God certainly gifted us in these areas to both be able to help with these needs, however we are both passionate about the capital C church. We are also both strategic thinkers with a variety of experience in multiple areas and facets of the church. We both had been worship leaders, lead pastors and held just about every other title in the church. We both had worked in rural and urban churches, in tiny towns and major metro cities. We both had experienced working in a church plant of six people and also the megachurch environment. We knew what it took to lead a successful church and rescue one that needs help, but of course that goes way beyond the physical side of things. We both knew that God gave us this type of Swiss Army knife, multi-faceted experience for a reason.

Those couple of days in Michigan lifted something out of both of us that set us on fire, even though it would be a couple of years before that came to fruition. We also learned on that trip something that we weren't really sure of before, that we worked really well together. It was unlike any ministry partnership that we had ever had. As John Maxwell says, "Teamwork makes the dreamwork." This rang true and proved that two is better than one when it comes to changing the world or impacting the church. We were not meant to be lone rangers in ministry and we discovered that we had immense amounts of fun making it happen. When you click with someone in ministry or in business, everything seems to just fit together perfectly.

In Ecclesiastes there is a passage that says,

"A person standing alone can be attacked and defeated, but two can stand back-to-back and conquer. Three are even better, for a triple-braided cord is not easily broken."

We were beginning to discover that together we could conquer so much more for God than if we were to go at it alone. It is much harder to be knocked down when you have strength in numbers and when God connects you to the right people. Strength is found when you work together to accomplish a vision. There is extreme power in the plural, as opposed to the singular.

That moment was the genesis of The Ministry Mechanics. The name would come later, but the idea to "build the church and equip the leader" was born on that trip. We knew other people were consulting churches and leaders, but we felt we could provide something with a different spin than others. Real talk from two guys who have done it. We aren't theologians, even though we are both pastors. We wanted to give super practical solutions for issues that leaders who are knee-deep in the trenches deal with on a daily basis. Those things aren't taught in seminary, but The Ministry Mechanics are well versed in the practical.

The Ministry Mechanics are plural for a reason, because we are stronger together. We feed off of each other's creative abilities and the collaboration spawns greater good for the Church. This happened through obedience and the awareness of the need for each other. Something incredible happens in your life, when your blade continues to be sharpened by others, when you are challenged to become better than you ever could be by yourself. If you don't have that in your life, is it possible you are missing out on the full calling God has on you?

As a leader, maybe you are struggling every week, just hoping people will show up. Or perhaps you're thinking to yourself, "How are we going to make payroll or pay the bills?" We have felt those same pressures, and I promise you it's so much easier when you have someone to share those burdens and even the joys of ministry. Be sensitive to the promptings of the Holy Spirit and ask Him to send you the right person with the passion that matches your passion or maybe even pushes you further. God won't leave you alone, but you have to be willing to move and connect with others. When that happens, God will begin to order the planets that make up the right solar system around you and no matter your vantage point, it will be a beautiful thing. If you want to see something special happen through you, allow Him to put the right people in your life.

THAT AIN'T ME

CHAPTER 4

The Ministry Mechanics

"The two most important days in your life are the day you were born and the day you find out why." - Mark Twain

Leadership development experts before our generation would tell you to discover your weaknesses and personally develop yourself by making them stronger. There has been a major shift in that thinking over the last decade, especially with books such as *Strength Finders* from Gallup. The thinking now is to be competent in your weaknesses, but focus more on sharpening the strengths that God has given you. Don't waste time on trying to be a "ten" in an area that you only have the capability to be a "six." It will cause frustration when you can't achieve the ten and it will distract you from achieving the very thing God calls you to do.

We like to use the same logic for discovering and defining your dream. When you start eliminating the things you are not, it is easier to define who you are and what you are passionate about. When you focus on your passions, you will more than likely define your dream and purpose.

Many times on our way to lunch or to work on location, we would use a phrase that just stuck with us. It's probably not proper English, but that's ok, we are just two guys from Tennessee. If there was something that we didn't feel wired to do or something that didn't fit our vision, we just simply said, "THAT AIN'T ME." Which didn't mean we were too good for that idea or thing, but it meant we knew who we were and what we are wired to do. We knew if we wasted our time with anything outside of the spectrum of our God-given talents, we couldn't do it with the excellence it required to be successful and the heart to see it through to completion.

Once you discover who you are, it's time to seek God and allow Him to define the dream for your life. What is the thing you were created to do? Is it to plant a new church? Is it to be faithful in the church you are already in? Could God be embedding a vision in you to create a product that benefits the church and the world like the YouVersion Bible App? That idea simply came from a church and now it's having a major impact on not only the Church but has been downloaded hundreds of millions of times all over the world. Do you have a dream inside of you to launch a business but you never felt the timing was right? Whatever it may be for your life, God is always faithful to give you the proper tools to discover your passion. You just have to be aware of God's promptings when He is calling you to the very thing you are made to do.

Begin on Your Knees

Maybe you don't know where to start when it comes to defining your dream. The process always begins on your knees. Make no mistake, feelings are fleeting but God's guidance should be at the epicenter of every major decision of your life. Most great movements throughout history have begun with Godly leaders seeking the Holy Spirit's direction. We should align our purposes to God's will rather than hoping God's will somehow will align with our vision. Psalm 37:4 says, *"Take delight in the Lord, and he will give you your heart's desire."* We often misinterpret this Scripture and think that He will give us whatever we want, when in essence He wants for our hearts to be so intertwined with His that our desires align with His desires.

Many times we are too busy telling God what we want Him to do in our lives, that His voice is drowned out by our incessant need to be heard. What would happen if while we were allowing God to define the dream He has for us, we would sit down, stay quiet, be still and wait?

Let me be real with you, I (Jeremy) don't have the spiritual "gift" of patience. I am okay waiting in the doctor's office or in long lines (especially to ride an amazing roller coaster). Both of those have obvious conclusions. You finally get to see the doctor after two hours and you finally get to ride the ride for 2 minutes after waiting for 45. I personally struggle in the situations where the outcome isn't obvious or may be cloudy or when life throws a curve ball and stumps you. I want immediate action, immediate satisfaction and that is not always going to happen. To be completely transparent, those times freak me out and the people that see my reaction probably think I am losing my mind.

Maybe you can relate to this, maybe not. When I am waiting to hear from God, especially when I am waiting to receive God's guidance for the next step in life, the anxiety overwhelms me. When I don't have all the answers or if there is any uncertainty, it is unsettling. I try to talk my way out of it, I try to make sure everything is fine, because I want solutions, not uncertainty. I don't know if it's a guy thing, but I immediately go into fix-it mode to the point where people have to tell me there is nothing to fix, it just takes time. Can you relate? Or I am completely out on "freak out" island by myself?

We do live in an instant gratification world. I have turned into a "now" guy as well. The truth is we are not meant to have everything now and we are not meant to have all the answers all the time. We have to give God room to move in the situation. When we are defining the vision for our life, we have to be reminded that He can't work if we always have our hands on it. There is no room for His unseen hands. Here are three things to remember when you are hitting your knees and seeking God with everything in you:

1. Sit Down

Sometimes we need to sit down, stop pacing around worrying and give it over to Jesus completely. Your pacing isn't going to change anything. Instead of worrying, throw yourself into worship and put your focus on the only One who has the solution. Worship while you wait! When you worship while you wait, God prepares your heart for the promise that he's working on for you! You will not change one thing by worrying except for your mind and your heart to be more stressed and confused. You will take up the space that is rightfully God's! Along with worship, dive deeper in the Bible than ever before. During this time, if you will choose to focus on His Word, the words will leap off of the page and into your heart. If you want direction, the compass is His Word. Sit down in the waiting room as you seek Him!

2. Stay Quiet

Trust me, more words will not change your situation. In fact most of the time it will harm the situation. Instead of getting the answer you desire, you delay the process. Give it time. Do less talking and do more listening. Listen for the still small voice of God, because He is the only one that provides the direction that you need to move. Listen for the lesson that He is teaching you in the waiting room. That lesson is different for everyone. For me during a season of waiting, there are times when God is teaching me to relinquish control. He also could be preparing you for a new season by doing something inside of you before He does something through you. He's using the waiting room to shape us and mold us to be more like Him.

3. Be Still and Wait

Psalm 46:10 says, *"Be still, and know that I am God."* Basically what He is saying is, "relax and watch Me do My thing!" Waiting is hard because it requires extreme faith. Sometimes I think my faith is weak because I try to take matters into my own hands to get my way. I keep getting up from my chair in the waiting room, trying to do my thing and my thing alone never works. I can hear God say, "Sit down and let Me handle this!" Trusting God through trials, takes a dose of humility and complete reliance on Him. I would be lying if I told you that it was easy. In fact it's hard for me and it's going to be hard for you, but you have to let Him have the reins. He's got this!

All throughout Scripture, there is story after story of people being faithful, and it wasn't easy for them either. Joseph went from the pit to the prison to the palace. It took a while, but he found his purpose and God blessed him abundantly. But I am certain there were many times Joseph found himself sitting in the waiting room. In those moments, Joseph relied more on God than ever before. His relationship with the Father was legitimized and refined. God worked in His life throughout the process even before He gave him his purpose. It's in the process that God reveals His plan to you. Don't be so busy looking for His plan that you miss out on His process.

No matter how long your wait is, it's worth it, so don't give up. God knows your heart and every single desire of your heart, so let Him align your heart with His. Above all, the consummate bond between you and God will be solidified in the waiting and you will have full clarity of the direction He is leading you and the dream that He has birthed in you.

Fasting

"When we seek God with fasting and prayer, He always shows up" - John Wesley

This quote has been true in my (Jeremy) life. Most of the major steps in my life have been preceded by a season of fasting and every time I have fasted, God has shown up in a major way. It is still evident today that prayer and fasting unlocks something within us and provides answers to our questions. Now let me be clear, my prayers aren't always answered the way I want them to be answered, but the answers come. At times we give God an option, which is laughable if you think about it. "God open the doors that need to be opened and close the doors that need to be shut." I will have to be transparent, there are doors that I give God "permission" to shut that I don't want shut, but I pray that prayer anyway. When that door closes, even though it may be the one you didn't want shut, it provides clarity.

When you are trying to define God's dream for your life, fasting drowns out the noise of your world. It allows you to focus entirely on God and His plan for your future. Through a season of fasting you can define the dream that God puts on your heart and the puzzle pieces fall into place. You may be saying "well this is a no-brainer, of course fasting works." The problem is many of us know the power of fasting however we refuse to tap into its full power in our lives. Fasting is not always easy, it takes discipline and a willingness to fully submit to God.

What Keeps You Up at Night?

Craig Groeschel once asked two questions that really stuck with me: "What makes you angry?" and "What keeps you up at night?" He wasn't talking about someone cutting you off in traffic or stubbing your toe on a coffee table. He was talking about an injustice that left your soul unsettled and caused a fire within your belly. A passion that wouldn't be settled until you did something about it and a burden that prompted you to action.

After you have prayed and fasted, it's time to ask yourself the tough questions. What are you passionate about? There is a good chance that God has given you that burden and that fire for a reason, so don't ignore that prompting and the fire within. Pray that God gives you this sincere longing deep within your soul and the ability to begin the process of doing your part.

For The Ministry Mechanics, after we internally asked those questions, we knew that helping churches and leaders is really what kept us up at night. Several years ago someone asked me the question, what will the church look like in 20 years? I simply said, small, if we don't make changes. 10,000 churches disappeared in the United States in a 5 year period, they just shut their doors. 80% of 14-33 year olds said church is not important to them. These startling statistics weigh heavily on us, but we don't want to be sad and do nothing about it. That is what drives us to do what we do and to reverse the trend that we are seeing.

We don't want the church in America to become museums or shrines of faith of years gone by, but a thriving, living organism of life change. That is what keeps us up at night. That is what drives us to do whatever it takes to bring change to the world and reverse the statistics. What burden keeps you awake? What drives you?

When you discover that, you will be on your way to defining you dream.

Good vs. God

When you are dreaming and seeking God's will for your life, at times it's difficult to discern between good ideas and God ideas. Even though there is a difference of only one letter between the two, the real difference is life-altering. Good ideas are a dime-a-dozen. God ideas are anointed and have the ability to change lives around you and change the world.

If you are a leader and you are making a major decision, it would be good to use this same filter. Our churches today are tempted to chase every good idea, whether it's the next 40 days of something or a catchy slogan or #hashtag. The church news cycle and social media move so quickly today, we don't have time to slow our roll and ask God if He's in it or not. We assume that if it works for one church, it must be God's plan for ours. This couldn't be further from the truth. God doesn't want you to copy and paste the vision He has given someone else. While some things may work for your church and may be a good fit for your flock, many times we are trying to squeeze the old square peg in the round hole. At times we don't think about how this "good" idea may be overshadowing the God ideas that only He can place in our hearts. Don't miss the dream that God is giving you to chase the dream that doesn't belong to you.

Many times leaders can forget the God-sized vision that they were originally given because they are distracted by the overwhelming onslaught of good ideas. There is nothing wrong with good ideas, just be sure to not choose the good thing over the God thing. God will give you His vision and He will provide clarity when the time is right. When this happens, the God-sized vision will rise to the surface and you will have zero doubts about the direction that He is leading you. God's vision for your life will be greater than any recycled version of someone else's dream.

Remember Your Why?

Maybe you have already defined your dream. Perhaps you did that many years ago. But maybe God is doing something new in your life. Maybe you have forgotten your why and just need to be reminded. That God-given passion, purpose and fire that once burned brightly just needs to be rekindled. Or maybe, just maybe your why is changing, which is very common.

Why do you do what you do? If it's for the wrong reasons, it won't last, you will get burned out. Is it for the pat on the back? Is it to be noticed and recognized? Is it to feel good about yourself? We are all human and those things make us feel like a million bucks, but those reasons shouldn't be the reason we do it. The reason should be simply because we have a desire to honor God's calling on our lives and to make an impact on others, and to see people take the step from death to life.

If you are not doing what you are doing to honor God's unique calling on your life, step out and step back into what God is calling you to immediately. Take a season to re-evaluate your calling because God is evidently working on your heart and could be bringing you into a new season and it's likely that He is doing a new thing in your life. It's been said, that if you are serving in a ministry that you don't feel called to, you are taking the spot of someone else that really is called to do that very thing. It's easy to keep the fire going if the fire isn't manufactured, but rather ignited by the Holy Spirit. Check your priorities and make sure they are aligned with the purposes of God.

Are You Stuck?

If you are a leader or pastor, you have felt the pressure of leading an organization or church and have probably felt stuck. You might even be stuck right now. Maybe you are unaware that you are stuck and frankly that could be the most vulnerable and dangerous place to be. You have a hit a wall and you haven't noticed because you are so overwhelmed with the day-to-day of keeping the organization afloat. The lights are on and the bills have been paid one more month and you fall back into the trap of living like that again this month. It's a vicious cycle that is very difficult to stop.

For some of you, you have run out of ideas and the things you were doing to grow the church 10 years ago are failing to work. You have been through every program and strategy that everyone has put out and the well is dry. You have stressed over it and you just don't know what your next move is going to be. These are very real frustrations and anxieties that are faced by many pastors and leaders who just want to make the Gospel of Jesus known to more people. I would say this is where a majority of our pastors in America today are living. I want to assure you this is not where God wants you to live. He doesn't want you to simply survive another month being a leader or pastor. He wants you to thrive in your calling and change the world wherever you are planted. At the Ministry Mechanics we want to help you take your church to the next level. We don't want your church to be stagnant and go years without producing new life. We also don't want you as the leader to be disengaged and just drawing a paycheck. If you have hit what seems to be a dead end, there is hope for you but you can't stay the way you are and expect things to change.

Here are three key questions that you need to ask if you are indeed stuck and don't know where to turn:

1. Are you still called to this church or organization?

Being stuck sometimes is a direct correlation to a lack of vision. The vision always flows from God. So if you feel the flow of vision has dried up, ask God for a fresh, anointed vision. If you have done this, maybe the question should be, am I still called to lead this place? Only God can give you refreshing, life-giving vision and He's also the only One who can answer that question. Spend some time with God alone, away from any distractions and allow Him to speak into your life. This question must be answered before any others are introduced.

2. Are you willing to change?

This is a tough one, because as a leader at times we don't think we have to change. We may even be oblivious to change, because we think that what we are doing is working. If you aren't experiencing transformation, then whatever you are doing simply isn't working. If your church has become inwardly focused, then the culture must change and you have to be willing to let go of some control to see that culture change. Sometimes drastic, bold risks need to be taken to bring about change. Are you going to be the leader that is willing to take those necessary steps? We want to encourage you to keep reading because we will be touching on these steps in a later chapter.

3. Are you willing to reach out for help?

We can't do ministry alone, sometimes we need to humble ourselves and ask for help. That's what the Ministry Mechanics are all about: helping churches reach their goals and true potential. We are an organization that specializes in church growth and getting leaders unstuck. If you really feel called to the place you are serving and you are willing to change, we would love to partner with you to bring about change in your church and community. Our desire is to see leaders across the country find the sweet spot of ministry and not to be miserable. Let us help you have an impact on the Kingdom!

Make Sure You Have Plenty of Elbow Room

When you get to the place where you can truly define the dream God has placed on your heart, then it's time to buckle in because God is about to do great things in you and through you. This passage always brings to mind that when you step out, God is faithful and His best is yet to come.

"Sing, barren woman, who has never had a baby.
  Fill the air with song, you who've never experienced childbirth!
You're ending up with far more children
  than all those childbearing women." God says so!
"Clear lots of ground for your tents!
  Make your tents large. Spread out! Think big!
Use plenty of rope,
  drive the tent pegs deep.
You're going to need lots of elbow room
  for your growing family.
You're going to take over whole nations;
  you're going to resettle abandoned cities.
Don't be afraid—you're not going to be embarrassed.
  Don't hold back—you're not going to come up short."
Isaiah 54:1-4 MSG

How big are your dreams? I assure you that God's dream for you is bigger than your own. This scripture is not just talking about giving birth to a baby. This passage is saying that we need to prepare for the harvest. Plan and prepare because God is about to bless you beyond your wildest expectations. He will blow your mind with depth that you have never seen. We have to dream big and make sure that we have plenty of elbow room. As DL Moody once said, "If God is your partner, make your plans BIG." Discover which direction God is moving and move with Him.

LEAP TO THE DEEP

CHAPTER 5

THE MINISTRY MECHANICS

In 1998, a struggling business owner named Kendra Scott had lost her life savings and was forced to shut down her fashionable hat store in Texas. She began the store with the idea to meet a need for cancer survivors who were losing their hair due to chemo. Her stepfather was diagnosed with cancer, so this business really hit home for her. He was the one that gave her the money to get the business started and unfortunately lost his savings as well. Kendra felt like, in her words, "the biggest failure on the planet." She thought she had let everyone down. Kendra sulked for a moment and then decided to pick herself up and move forward in a positive way.

She knew that this wasn't the end and that something greater was in store for her. She was passionate about unique jewelry and fashion and even through failure discovered her true dream. The only thing left to do was to make the initial jump into the unknown, robust world of jewelry and fashion. Her vision was clear but it was audacious and bold. I'm sure she was saying to herself, "This is my moment, if I don't seize this very moment in time, I will be replaying it in my mind forever."

Kendra took her initial investment of $500 and bought the supplies to make the pieces of jewelry herself. She began making these pieces in her spare bedroom. When she had completed the samples of her designs, she would go around to jewelry stores with her newborn baby to pitch her vision and her brand. Most of these stores would say no, but a few made actual orders. The vision that was in her heart had to come to fruition; she was determined to make it happen. The business began to take off and soon there was a high demand for Kendra Scott jewelry.

Kendra's small little company, that began in her spare bedroom with her handcrafted jewelry pieces, would skyrocket to become a major hit and one of the fastest growing fashion companies ever. After just a few years, her initial $500 investment would somehow blossom into unthinkable numbers. Just a few months ago, it was reported that the company that started with no outside investments, was now worth over one billion dollars. The vision that started with one employee in a spare bedroom, now has over 2000 employees.

After her first company failed, she could very easily have given up and at the very least could've been gun shy to take such a bold leap of faith. This young entrepreneur took what she had learned from her first business failing and started over from scratch and did things the right way the next time around. There were bumps along the way, as there always are when doing something audacious. Maybe you can relate. If you are a leader who has experienced failures or mistakes in the past, this can be an encouragement to you. We can learn from our mistakes and move forward. You too can be successful the next time around, just as Kendra was.

She clearly shook off the past, defined the dream, gauged when the timing was right and began her journey by taking a calculated risk. Today, she is seeing an abundance of blessings because she decided to take that giant leap. Not only is she reaping the blessings, she is giving back in multiple ways through philanthropy.

There was another leap of faith that was significant. This leap wasn't just a small one and it's found in Scripture. In Luke chapter 5, Jesus is standing on the shore of Lake Gennesaret and the crowd was pushing toward Him, just trying to hear the Word of God. Scripture tells us:
"Jesus noticed two boats tied up. The fishermen had just left them and were out scrubbing their nets. He climbed into the boat that was Simon's and asked him to put out a little from the shore. Sitting there, using the boat for a pulpit, he taught the crowd. When he finished teaching, he said to Simon, "Push out into deep water and let your nets out for a catch."
Luke 5:1-11 MSG

Simon's first reaction to Jesus' commands was an excuse. He told Jesus that they had been out all night and hadn't caught hardly anything. He then relented and said if you say so, I will let down the nets. As soon as he said those words, the fish were filling the nets. The nets were so full of fish that it was putting a strain on them and they were about to snap. So much so that they had to wave for someone to come over and help with the haul.

Many times that is our natural reaction to God's instructions, we make excuses. We may even give God what we think is a better idea. Then eventually we will give in and do it His way and we see the abundance of His blessings in our life. The key to the instruction of Jesus to Simon was that he requested for him to push out into the deep water. The deep water isn't always the safest place and it's not always the most comfortable. If you have ever been deep sea fishing, you know how it feels to be in the open water. At times it feels lonely, helpless and it can even be frightening.

God calls us to the place where there is no safety net or life preserver because He is the ultimate preserver and we are never alone, He is there with us. In Isaiah 43:2 God promises us, "When you go through deep waters, I will be with you." He calls us to a deeper place so we can visualize what only He can see for us. A reward that outweighs the risk, but we must push out to the deepest parts of the water to witness
it. By this simple act of obedience, our nets are filled to capacity and we can't even contain the blessings that come our way.

Craig Groeschel says, *"To step toward your destiny, you have to step away from your security."*

If you want to do what God has called you to do, sometimes it requires you to do some things that may be uncomfortable. Sometimes it doesn't make sense to the rest of the world. God never gives you a dream that matches logic or your bank account. Your dream is in direct correlation to the size of your faith. If you have shallow faith, it won't have much of a return but if you choose to have deep faith the full blessing will come to fruition.

What Are You Waiting On?

"By faith Abraham when called to go...obeyed and went, even though he did not know where he was going." Hebrews 11:8

I love the quote that says, *"Chase down your passion like it's the last bus of the night."* We should have a sense of urgency that if we don't take the next step of obedience we will miss out what God desires for our lives. Remember that delayed obedience is direct disobedience and I don't know about you but I don't want to be out of step with where God is leading me.

The stakes are too high for you not to leap to the deep. You can't afford to take it slow when it comes to His direction. Abraham didn't say, "Can you give me a map?" God just told him to go and for Abraham to trust Him every step of the way. Many of us are waiting on God to move, when He is saying, "Make the first move and I will bless your obedience." If you are waiting until you have it all together, then you will never leap to the deep. In Ecclesiastes 11:4-6 it says, *"Farmers who wait for perfect weather never plant."* If you are waiting for the timing to be just right, you may miss out on what God truly wants for your life. It's the age old principle that when we can afford it, we will get married or have kids. While that's a noble theory, life never works out that way. Someday tends to turn into never. When God calls, go and allow Him to guide your future.

The beginning of the journey, begins with one step! God is calling everyone to do something, and if you are going to go on this new adventure with God, you can't stay where you are! It's a lot easier to step out, but harder to keep going once you've stepped out. God will give you everything you need to be successful and the perseverance to continue the journey. God is faithful and blesses our obedience. He will always provide a way. Believe in the exciting adventure that He calls you to and never for one minute doubt His voice and His hand on you.

If we saw everything that God was going to do in our life, we couldn't handle the reality of our future. We probably would try to put the brakes on it because of our own insecurities or fear. God has the ability to see the entire master puzzle that makes up our life; we don't have that luxury or viewpoint. He only asks us to lay down one piece of the puzzle at a time in obedience.

If you have ever been on Google Earth, you have seen the different viewpoints. God has the aerial view and sees everything that surrounds us and what is coming up ahead. We are given the street view of our lives, which is limited but clear. If we truly trust God like we claim to, then we will trust Him enough to allow Him to navigate us through each step of the journey. He promises to be a lamp unto our feet and a light unto our path. Believe that promise and live your life in the illuminated path rather than in the darkness of disobedience.

Arrows Will Fly

Brace yourself because once you take the leap to the deep, not everyone will be on board with your decision and some people probably won't understand your vision. Sometimes it's the people that we care about the most, at times your own family, who won't necessarily get it. That's alright because God didn't give this vision to them; He gave it to you. If God has asked you to take the leap to the deep, don't let anyone or anything stand in your way. As God begins to bless this vision, others will begin to see why you felt so strongly about this vision before the leap.

We recently saw an interesting interview with Elon Musk of Space X and Tesla fame. The interviewer was asking Elon about the detractors that he had from the space community. Famous astronauts of yesteryear had been his strongest naysayers. These men were his heroes and inspired him to do the very thing that they were criticizing him for. As he responded to his heroes' criticism, he was visibly choked up. You could tell that he took it to heart. Sometimes the people that inspire you to do the thing that you are called to do won't be with you. That's ok, they can't fully comprehend the scope of your calling, because it's not theirs, it's yours.

Some folks may jump on the bandwagon later in the game. They won't necessarily be on board in the beginning but they might eventually catch the vision. Lovingly engage these people with grace and allow them to humbly join the ride. This is one of the many reasons to never burn bridges with people, because who knows who might show back up in your life.

Not only will people in your sphere of influence not get it, there may be those who do not know you throwing arrows your way. I remember when I planted a church twelve miles from a church that I had previously worked. Shortly after I announced my intentions, I had lunch with an older mentor and he warned me to get ready because the arrows would fly in my direction. Anytime you take a leap to do something audacious for God, the enemy takes it personally and he likes to use people as a stumbling block along the way.

Spiritual warfare will take place prior to your leap and will condemn you on the back end after the leap. The enemy will do everything he can to prevent you from succeeding but thankfully our success is up to God. Our only responsibility is to be obedient and steadfast throughout the process. There will be haters along the way, but don't listen to the chatter of the ones who don't have your best interest in mind. Put people around you that will support you and encourage you along the way. I'm not talking about just yes people, I'm speaking of the people who see your heart and will run alongside you without hesitation. No matter what, don't be crushed by criticism but allow God's opinion to have the only vote.

Move With the Movers

Many years ago I(Jeremy) remember hearing Pastor Ed Young share a story of the time that his best friend left his church. Imagine how devastating that must've been, that your own best friend wouldn't be on board with your vision. Which is a great reminder that the people that will start with you, may not be the people that you end up with. When you leap to the deep cannonball style and go all in, there may be those who stay on shore. You may even unfortunately lose friends, but that shouldn't throw you off course or prevent you from leaping.

When I was planting a church, a friend of mine gave me great advice, he told me to move with the movers. You will go through seasons, where others will get stagnant and some will be on fire. To see continued growth, you must move with the movers and not get dragged by the ones who are checking out. Sometimes the people that will take you from A to B, may not be the ones that are along for the ride from B-Z. That doesn't mean that you won't love and support those who were there in the beginning. They just might not be called to go where God is taking you and you have to be at peace with that.

There was a great giving family that decided to leave the church. I was a young senior pastor so I was concerned. I had a conversation with a mentor and he told that God always blesses faithfulness. He taught me the law of replenishment: If one family leaves, God will send three more to replace them in your church. I struggled to believe that because I took losing a family to heart but I had to look at the big picture. My mentor was right. Within just a few weeks, three more families replaced the one family that decided to leave.

When you leap to the deep, leap with faith, not with fear. You must have confidence that no matter the circumstances around you, it should never trump the burning desire within you, given by God. Have faith that, no matter what, when you leap to the deep, He will be the one that keeps you afloat.

Shortly before my(Jeremy) son's third birthday, we went out on a boat in the lake for the day. Both of my kids had always loved water since they were born. On this day Skyler waterskied for the very first time and stayed up on the skis for several hundred yards before he fell. That little guy had absolutely zero fear being out on the open water. He never thought about the "what ifs" like his dad did. I was thinking
of all of the worst case scenarios and was frankly scared to death for him. He was cooler than the other side of a pillow.

What would happen if we took a leap to the deep with reckless abandon like he did that day? What if we chose to believe that God is the God of immeasurably more and He who began a good work in us will be faithful to complete it? He won't leave us stranded on an island. If He calls us to it, He will bless us accordingly. So take the leap to the deep and watch God move in your life.

Detours Can Be God Things Too

One day in December I (Jeremy) was driving from Knoxville to Chattanooga, where I was living at the time, when I got a call from Chris. He asked if I would be willing to consider coming on staff at a megachurch where he was working. At the time, I was seeking my next step in ministry and I was open to a change. I told Chris that I would certainly pray about it and see where God leads us.

What Chris didn't know was that just 15 minutes earlier on that same drive, I was crying out to God telling Him to open the doors that needed to be open and close the doors that needed to be slammed shut. I always expect God to answer and move, but I didn't expect him to move that quickly. In the instant gratification society that we live in today, that kind of response would fit nicely, but unfortunately it rarely happens that way.

Over the next few weeks we went through the interview process and within a couple of months I was moving to the great state of Texas. I got hired on as the Missions Pastor. In the year that I was there Chris and I did some of the more rewarding and successful things that we've done in ministry. However it became clear after a few months that the vision of the church didn't fit with our vision for ministry. It wasn't a bad vision, it just wasn't the vision that God had called us to.

Sometimes you will decide to take a leap of faith to discover that the vision isn't for you. Does that mean you made a bad decision? No, but God will allow us to go through a detour to teach us valuable lessons on the journey. We sometimes begrudge God for not allowing a situation to work out. I could've easily said, "God I wasted a whole year in a place where I didn't fit." But of course He would gently remind that there is always purpose in the detour.

God knew I needed to be in Texas to work closely with Chris so we could define our dream. That dream became the Ministry Mechanics and this detour gave us the necessary push to make it happen.

The detour is part of God's master plan to get you exactly where you need to be. Many times we mistake detours as mistakes when in essence it really isn't a detour to God. It's just a simply a different way than we had planned to go. We can always trust God through the detours of ministry and life.

In Exodus chapter 13, God took the Israelites through a detour even though it wasn't the shortest path.

"God did not lead them on the road through the Philistine country, though that was shorter. . . . God led the people around by the desert road toward the Red Sea."

We all know what happened at the Red Sea. God split the waters in two so the Israelites could pass through on dry land and the enemy was thwarted. God knew exactly what He was doing and the Israelites needed to trust Him completely with their lives. He planned a detour to not only help them reach their destiny but to protect them from the enemy.

Whether you are taking the leap for the first time or if you are discovering a whole new direction, God always knows the best route for you to take. Be fearless, trust Him and leap!

ALL NIGHT HUSTLE

CHAPTER 6

THE MINISTRY MECHANICS

Chapter 6 - All Night Hustle

"Make the most of every chance you get. These are desperate times!"
Ephesians 5:16 MSG

God warns us that we are living in desperate days and we must choose to redeem our time by carrying out the vision God has called us to. The alternative is that we can fall to the temptation like so many others have throughout time by squandering this opportunity and this vision that He has generously given. Consider the athlete who have all of the God-given talent in the world but find ways to waste it and never reach their full potential. Some people who are given a gift and choose to do nothing with it. It makes you wonder why they never applied it. I don't know about you, but I don't want to be another story of someone who has been given so much and done so little with it. Luke 12:48 says, *"Great gifts mean great responsibilities; greater gifts, greater responsibilities!"*

You each have been entrusted with so much but what will you do with what you are given? Will you sacrifice for it and do what it takes and at what cost? Will you seize the opportunity that God so graciously presents to you and do everything you can to follow His lead?

Once we leap to the deep, we sometimes expect God to bless us without doing the necessary work that is required of us. We think the work is done once we take the leap into the great unknown. The truth is, the work is just beginning. We can't take the brave leap of faith and then wait on God to bless us without fulfilling our end of the calling. He won't bless your laziness and lack of planning. If you are faithful and diligent with your part, God will always do His part. We must work like the results are up to us, knowing all along that the results are in God's hands.

Many of us want the blessings but we don't want to put in the hustle. (Let me pause right there and mention that when we say the word **hustle**, we don't mean shortcut, swindle or smooth talk, we simply mean putting in the maximum effort that God requires of us. Ok continue reading). I saw a sign once that said, the dream is free but the hustle is sold separately. God blesses us all by giving us a dream in our heart, but we have a choice by our own free will to do something with that dream or not.

Some of us do just enough to squeeze by, which is hard to understand. If you knew God had an audacious vision for your life, wouldn't you do everything in your power to accomplish that vision and make it a reality? The Apostle Paul tells in Colossians 3:22b: *"Don't just do the minimum that will get you by. Do your best!"* I want to accept that challenge every single day of my life and I want that for you as well. Put that passage on your desk in your office or tape it to your dashboard in your car. Hopefully that will encourage you to give maximum effort, put in the time, and give absolutely every ounce of your heart to fulfilling God's plan for your life.

When we were just beginning The Ministry Mechanics, we worked some long hours and even pulled some all nighters during that season of ministry. We knew that anything worth doing tends to be uphill and it was going to require everything we had to push it to the top. Quick bursts of hustle are required to accomplish the audacious. We would go to this place called The House of Pies in Houston. We would take our laptops and notepads and we would just hammer things out. We would dream and brainstorm, but then we would actually put the pen to the paper and begin to do the work that needed to be done. We accomplished so much in those early days because A.) God was blessing our obedience of leaping to the deep and B.) we were not just putting in the minimum required to be successful. We knew that we were representing Jesus Christ and we wanted to go all in with Him. Jesus said, *"If someone demands that you go one mile, go with him two miles"* (Matthew 5:41). Exceed what's expected of you, and watch God bless it.

Doers vs. Dreamers

Someone once told me (Jeremy) that I was a dreamer. I immediately responded by saying that I was a doer. It probably came off a bit defensive, but I had already come to realize that there is a big difference between a dreamer and a doer. Dreamers talk about what they are going to do one day. Doers actually stop talking about it and start walking toward doing the very thing that was put on their heart. God doesn't bless your talking, but He will bless your walking. Proverbs 14:23 says, *"All hard work brings a profit, but mere talk leads only to poverty."* In life you can be a dreamer *and* a doer, but more importantly God is looking for dreamers that do. Someone who will accept the call and put the hammer to the nail.

Let me be clear, it's completely natural to have dreams as long they don't stay dreams. God puts a dream in your heart for it to become a reality, not for it to remain a pretty picture in your head. It's like the sports talk show host that says this year's team is great on paper. Which means the team sounds amazing but we won't actually know if they are or not until they play the game. God is telling you that yes on paper you have potential, the sky is the limit with what you can accomplish, however it can't end there. You must choose to get in the game. Our hands must get dirty to become the doer that God wants us to be.

Many people in ministry today don't want to get their hands dirty. Those types of people want the titles and the authority but we don't want to pay the dues necessary to make it happen. Doers get their hands dirty and do jobs that sometimes aren't the most fun. My friend Brian Powell said recently that, "If you aren't willing to clean the toilets, you're not ready to lead the church." I would agree with that assessment. This doesn't mean we don't delegate responsibility, it just means at times we are the ones that need to push toward the prize and put in the sweat equity toward making this dream a reality. We are the ones who have been challenged by God to lead the way and be the model, even if it means humbling ourselves to clean toilets. By doing this you are becoming more like

Christ and that is the ultimate model of servant leadership. If serving is beneath you, then leadership is beyond you.

For over 20 years, we have both spent a majority of that time being GSD leaders in ministry. You are probably thinking, what is GSD? It simply stands for: "Get Stuff Done!" It means not stopping until the task gets completed, no matter how long it takes. We might even have to say no to some things we love to be able to say yes to things we love even more. That's the type of leader that God wants you to become if you are not already. That is also the type of person that you want on your team. A go-getter who doesn't make excuses and accomplishes a task when needed. What would happen if you built a team full of GSD leaders? One thing is for sure, you would get stuff done!

Act Like an Entrepreneur

Since we launched The Ministry Mechanics, our team has been creating, building, dreaming and living the lives of people who are trying to create something from nothing! These ideas about how to strengthen churches and equip leaders have been in our heads or have been manifesting themselves in random ways over the years. But now things are different. Now it's real. Now it's about organizing thoughts, clarifying purpose, developing strategies and formulating a plan.

Throughout the process, we've been reminded that startups are so different from established organizations. The life of a church planter is vastly different from that of a leader of an existing church. Any momentum that shows up in the early stages of launching something new is because a team is so committed to creating movement of any kind.

When you're launching a new work, you'll come up with out of the box innovations and incredibly bright ideas out of pure necessity. You'll take risks to build an audience. You'll get creative to find cost-effective methods of sharing your message with the world. You'll celebrate anyone who is willing to come alongside you to help bring your vision to reality. You'll actually rejoice when someone sends you an email wanting more information or likes your social media pages. This leads to rapid growth, strong word of mouth marketing and real movement toward your organizational goals.

On the flip side, leaders at established organizations tend to play it safe to avoid controversy. You'll dismiss innovations and creativity to stick with what brought you this far. You'll focus energy on your current customers/members. You'll overlook capable leaders with loads of potential within your organization, or worse, stick with leaders who haven't had a brilliant or creative thought in years. You'll bemoan emails from customers/members and loathe responding to the hundreds of social media interactions. This leads to slowed growth, mediocre word of mouth and stagnation toward organizational goals.

Nate Leung has a great graphic that illustrates some of the differences between employees and entrepreneurs.

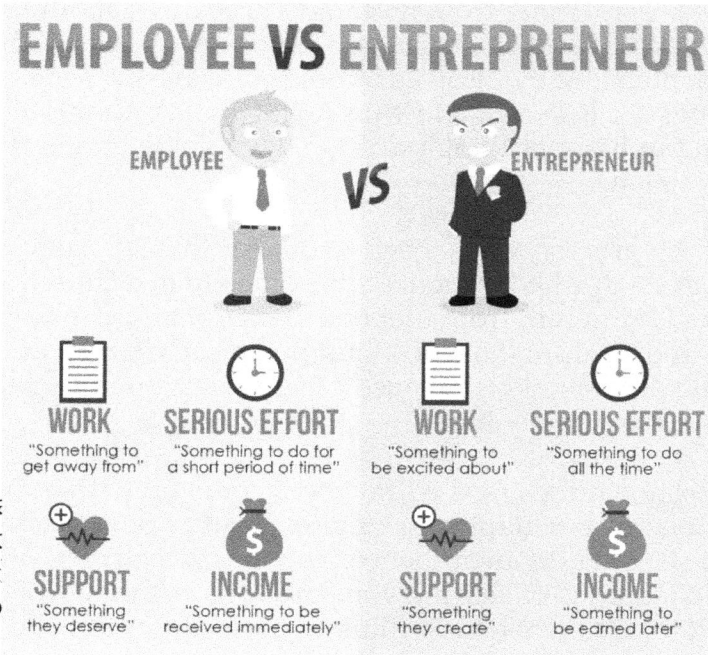

EMPLOYEE VS ENTREPRENEUR

EMPLOYEE   VS   ENTREPRENEUR

WORK — "Something to get away from"
SERIOUS EFFORT — "Something to do for a short period of time"
WORK — "Something to be excited about"
SERIOUS EFFORT — "Something to do all the time"

SUPPORT — "Something they deserve"
INCOME — "Something to be received immediately"
SUPPORT — "Something they create"
INCOME — "Something to be earned later"

You c..stors. How ....can we keep t..astructure to sup

Here are 3 tips to living like an entrepreneur:

1. Get Fired Up

This sounds so simple, but growth and vision starts with your passion for your product, organization and calling! If you're not excited, no one else will be. Passion is contagious. Energy is infectious. Remember that an organization feeds off of the energy of the leader. If you are at a low energy level, your team will reflect that same energy. You must be passionate about what you do. If you aren't, maybe it's time to examine what you're doing. Maybe it's time to get out of your current situation and lean into your passion. Work is always going to be challenging and difficult, but it can't be deflating and without merit. Finding the "why" in your "what" will go a long way to sustaining your success and energy in your current calling. Don't let anyone else have more vision for your community than you do. Be a motivator, encourager and leader who has passion and purpose in their work.

2. Prepare For The Future

Every good leader needs to leave some space in the work week for dreaming and visioneering. When was the last time you thought about your future, about what's next for your organization? Each week, devote some meaningful time to explore your community. Find the needs and create ways to meet them through your service. If you're only putting out fires and dealing with the present, you'll never move beyond the now. Good leaders are always looking to the future and finding new ways to grow their churches, engage customers or help change the world.

3. Give It Away

One of the best ways to get some time to think about what's next is to give away responsibility. Empowering capable leaders within your organization is a critical step toward growing your organization. Get out of your office and invest in the talent around you! Ask people about their passions and what they love about their jobs. Empower them to become leaders with real responsibility and decision-making power. Craig Groeschel reminds us that if we can find anyone in our organization that can accomplish our job, or parts of it, at 70% of our efficiency, it's time to give it away. Divide the workload, delegate responsibility and define the win. Spend time assessing challenges and celebrating the wins.

"Most leaders delegate tasks instead of authority. If you delegate tasks, you create followers. If you delegate authority, you create leaders." **Craig Groeschel**

Maybe it's been a while since you worked like an entrepreneur. This week, find a simple way to switch from thinking like an employee and try to work like an entrepreneur. Inspire some change and momentum in your organization. By keeping a startup mentality, it will breathe life into your processes and passions. Better still, you'll see more people cross the line of faith and get deeper into it. Remember the reason you started your church, business or organization in the first place, regain that original passion that pushed you to hustle and lean into it. Pray that God reignites that passion within you.

"Work willingly at whatever you do, as though you were working for the Lord rather than for people. Remember that the Lord will give you an inheritance as your reward, and that the Master you are serving is Christ." **Colossians 3:23-24**

At the end of our journey in life, we will have to give testimony to our story. We won't give God our resume for Him to look over because He will know every single thing we have ever done. I don't know about you, but I want to stand tall on that day and be proud that I poured every bit of my time, talent and treasure out to Him. Will you have a clear conscience that you did everything you could to build the Kingdom of God and to fulfill the vision He gave you? I want you to utilize every single gift and resource inside of you before your time is up. God uniquely wired you to lead; you were set apart for the path He has given you. Now you must choose to live a life filled with absolutely no regrets. Through hard work that honors God, He will honor your hustle and will bless you accordingly. Push through to the end and whatever you do, don't stop even if it takes all night.

THE HEALTHY LEADER

CHAPTER 7

THE MINISTRY MECHANICS

In the last chapter we talked about short bursts of hustle. In this chapter we will explore how to do that and keep the rest of your life in tact as well by becoming the healthiest leader possible. John Maxwell said recently that he doesn't believe in balance. There will be seasons where you will be out of balance, it's inevitable. There will be seasons where you will have to push hard to start the very thing God has placed inside of you. There will be other seasons that you will have to pour more into your family than normal. Be careful with this statement because it could easily be misinterpreted. This doesn't mean abandon your family when you are in the trenches of your calling and adversely it doesn't mean abandon your calling when your family needs you more. The pendulum will swing ever slightly one way or the other at times, but that means that either train shouldn't completely derail in the meantime. This season won't last forever, so don't lose focus of everything else in your life and abandon one thing for the other.

There are so many in ministry who are feeling the after effects of being burned out. One of the definitions of burnout is to be *depleted or drained due to overwork or stress."* This occurs in ministry much too often. We talk to leaders daily that are at their wits' end and have checked out emotionally, mentally, physically and many times even spiritually. They have given everything of themselves and they have nothing left in the tank. This doesn't just happen to pastors, but great volunteers and staff members that pour everything out until there is nothing left to pour to the people that matter the most. It leaves them pondering the question, "Is ministry even worth it anymore?"

What starts out as burnout sometimes leads to fizzle out. There are some that go past the point of no return and completely leave ministry. I have so many friends who I started ministry with, that have chosen a different career path. Some who now don't even attend a church, let alone work in one. That's when we begin to see heartbreaking statistics like this:

50% of pastors starting out today will not be in ministry in 5 years

89% of pastors have seriously considered leaving it

77% of pastors do not feel they have a good marriage

Only 1 in 10 pastors retire in ministry

We must do something to prevent this from becoming more of an epidemic than it already is. We must find ways to reverse these statistics.

You Can't Lead On Empty

A while back, I (Jeremy) woke up to the surprising news that a well-known pastor in Tennessee had resigned after 14 years of leadership. I watched him address the church that he loves and as I watched I couldn't help but see the anguish in his eyes. It's hard to leave a church that you love, trust me I know. As I was broken and tired several years ago, I stepped away from my church that I started and loved dearly. I knew my family needed my utmost attention and I knew that my family was my first ministry and priority.

As the pastor announced his resignation he said, "We've said that this is a church where it's okay to not be okay, and I'm not okay. I'm tired. And I'm broken and I just need some rest." It takes a huge dose of humility to admit that you are broken and to admit that your priorities have been off kilter. It takes a tremendous amount of courage to leave a place that you helped create and a place that is such a big part of who you are. My hope for this pastor is that the love of God's people will overwhelm him and his family during this time. I pray that the big C church is the big "C" church and wraps their arms around them and doesn't abandon them. I know that church will always do that, it's an amazing place, but I am calling out for the rest of us who call ourselves Christians to love on these pastors and leaders with the same embrace.

We tend to jump to conclusions when we hear news like this. I want to warn you to not bother with trying to figure out what went wrong in this situation or every other situation for that matter. Our only response should be love, leave the judging and convicting to others. As a wise man once said, "It's God's responsibility to judge, the Holy Spirit's job to convict and it's our job to love." Pondering about what happened or how could it have been prevented doesn't help the pastor or his family who are both broken. Just give them the space, grace and love that they desperately need during this time. Simply pray for healing, restoration and renewal in their lives.

With that said, my array of emotions were on a roller coaster ride since that day when I heard the news, especially when it hit so close to my own situation. I ran the emotions of anger, frustration and sadness. But most importantly, I have a burden for leaders who are burned out, broken and have lost the passion to even serve. I remember being at my lowest point and I received a message from none other than the same pastor who resigned from burnout. He just wanted to tell me he was praying for me and he encouraged me to continue to fight on. It breaks my heart that this pastor needs that type of message today.

I'm sure he has been surrounded with so many people who love him, which is an amazing thing. But what happens to the guy who doesn't have support like that? What if he leaves a church that doesn't have as much grace as his did? Who loves on those leaders? Unfortunately I have seen hundreds of leaders leave the ministry. Good folks, yet imperfect people who have had a tremendous impact on the Kingdom. This has to stop!!! Churches and people have to change, so these people don't fall through the cracks.

So what do we do about this epidemic of pastors burning out or just flat out leaving the ministry? We have heard the statistics and they are gloomy. How do we prevent people from getting to this point? Here are a few things I learned when I took a break from ministry. I have gained some perspective that I didn't have when I was inside the church bubble. Now that I am back in ministry, I have learned to do things differently. Even when you do these things, it's still very difficult, because the enemy is out to steal, kill and destroy.

Unplug and Rest

"God created the universe in 6 days; he rested on the 7th. His message? "If creation didn't crash when I rested, it won't crash when you do!" - Max Lucado

Yes, I know this sounds easy, make no mistake, it is not. 4 hours of sleep isn't good for you, no matter who you ask. They are lying to you. No one can keep up with that pace. Turn your phone off and go to bed. There is nothing that you do at 2 am that can change anything in your church. If you have to do it at that hour, you need to re-evaluate your time management skills during the day.

Take Vacations

Yes that's right. If your church doesn't give you a decent amount of vacation, you may be at the wrong church. That needs to be a priority from day one before you sign on. The fact is, if you don't schedule your vacations, they won't happen. The same is true with off days and segments of time that you should dedicate to relaxation or family time.

The Church Isn't Your First Ministry, Your Family Is

If you don't get this one right, life will become very rocky. I can assure you of that. What would happen if we poured as much into our family as we do our church or ministry? We work all hours of the day and night to make sure we get the church just right. Do we put the same energy to make sure our family is just right? We could rescue our whole community and lose our family without noticing. Then it's not worth it. The word of God says that He will build His church. Be faithful and committed to your family first and God will bless the rest. I believe it's always great when your family does ministry together. Let them join in the mission and allow them to have a role in your calling. You are in this together for the long run. Instead of doing your thing separately and making them feel disconnected, become a team and watch God multiply your efforts. God may use that time together as a family to inspire your children into a calling of their own. You never know what He can do when you commit that family time to back Him.

You Can't Lead on E

There is not a vehicle in the world that will run on empty. You will eventually run out of fuel if you don't continuously recharge and renew your soul. Your creativity will begin to wane and people will begin to notice. Take a sabbatical and remove yourself from the situation before it's too late. If you are a leader that doesn't want to take a sabbatical because of your pride, then your church needs to have it built in and they should mandate it to protect you from yourself.

Take Care of Your Body

Ellison Research reports that according to the results of their study: 71% of pastors say that they are overweight by an average of 32.1 pounds, 52% say that they experience signs of stress on a weekly basis. These are both linked to high blood pressure, heart disease, strokes and other conditions that will cut your time on this Earth short. It is time you get serious about how you take care of yourself. You spend so much time caring and investing in others, that you get the leftovers, sometimes literally. It reminds me of the safety instructions on a flight. Be sure when the oxygen mask drops down to put it on yourself first, rather than your child. If you are dead, you can't help your child and it's useless. Same is true in ministry, if you don't take care of yourself first and foremost, then it will impossible to help anyone else. You can't reach the lost when you are dead. Make the change today when it comes to your physical well-being.

Transparent Leaders and Churches Filled with Grace

We as the big "C" church need to create a safe environment and build a culture for it to be okay for leaders not to be okay. That works both ways, the leader should feel comfortable being real and transparent but this can only happen when churches lovingly accept the leader for who they are. The church is the greatest conduit for grace, yet when our capacity for grace is put to the test, we revert back to judgment. I see a church that understands the need to protect and love the pastor and a pastor who feels he has total amnesty and honesty. What tends to happen is that we let the pastoral pride sink in and we feel that we can't be real with our people, because they won't understand and we will appear weak. We have this misconception that others will view us with a dent in our armor. We are not better than you or smarter than you, but we are one of you. Yes we are set apart for service, but gone are the days when pastors should be on a pedestal. We are human and flawed and it's time that we lead from our scars rather than from our perceived perfection.

Accountability

We can't do this alone nor should we want to do this alone. When we get alone on an island is when it becomes dangerous. We can't be effective when we are leading from a place of isolation. You must surround yourself with solid people who will encourage you, people who will ask the tough questions. If you don't have different points of view speaking into your life, you need to stop what you are doing now and rethink that structure. If you only have people around you that enable you or tell you what you want to hear then its time to get some different people in your life. They are doing more harm than good and you are allowing that to happen. Accountability is only as good as your willingness to be transparent.

Burnout and exhaustion aren't new in ministry. It's been around forever, but there are new variables in the church today that expose it on a new level. There is increasing pressure to keep up with the world, fill up the seats with people and become more and more relevant than we were the week before. It's a never ending rat race and an unrelenting treadmill that is unforgiving and seems to not have an off switch or a pause button. As leaders we feel if we don't keep up with the break neck pace, we will lose everything, our church (which isn't ours to lose), givers (not ours either) and our ministry (still not ours) and livelihood. The pressure is enormous and is impossible to live up to. The culture must change, there are too many good people falling by the wayside and eventually leaving ministry.

Part of our calling at The Ministry Mechanics is to keep pastors from making it to this point. I'm tired of seeing pastors who have lost their passion to serve and are sleepwalking through the rut of ministry and at times it's to their family's detriment. We have a desire to see leaders lead by no longer hiding their scars but rather by exposing them and allowing God to use them for good. God has the ability to take the very thing that the devil desperately uses to try to destroy us and changes others with the stories of our scars and wounds. He has done that with us and he wants to use you to do that as well.

I (Jeremy) was told immediately following the greatest storm of my life, that my greatest days of ministry are ahead of me and not behind by Chris. Having someone to encourage you is invaluable because they can see the forest for the trees that you are hiking through. I struggled to believe the encouragement but I see the fruit of that today. I believe that still for leaders who may feel tired, broken and hopeless. God did not bring you to this place without using it for His glory and for your good. If you are struggling, stop lying to yourself, drop the facade and admit it. Don't wait, it will only make things worse. I don't want to be just a guy who writes one chapter in a book about it, drops the bomb and leaves. I want to be a part of the solution and not the problem. So I am willing to help get leaders on the right path to healing and provide encouragement to you.

I wrote a book called *Unbroken, Discovering Wholeness Through the Shattered Pieces of Life*. It's a book that many pastors, leaders and anyone who has felt broken have read and have been helped. But I want to go a step further, I want to personally help you. If you are a leader or pastor who is feeling tired, broken and burned out due to any reason, I want to encourage you and talk to you. I am giving you my number, 713-492-5266 and my email jeremy@theministrymechanics.com. Feel free to drop me a line or call me at any time of the day. I don't want to see you go through the pain that so many of us had to go through. Let's stop this epidemic of running on empty, join with me as I pray for restoration over so many who are hurting in ministry today! May God give them a dose of humility, renew their soul, restore their homes and reignite their passion! Heal our broken world!

Some of you are just barely hanging on and have had thoughts of giving up and throwing in the proverbial towel. God didn't call you into this to abandon you. I want to encourage to keep fighting because God is not done with you.

Burnout Prevention

Many of us take vitamins to be healthy and stave away sickness because no one wants to get sick. We take preventative measures to make sure that our physical bodies stay in tact. We work out to get stronger and to stay healthy. If you want to do it right, we create a plan to better our health and by doing that we allow our bodies to stay healthy longer. We are giving ourselves longevity in this thing we call life.

As leaders we should take the same preventative measures with the people in our care, not just with their physical bodies but their emotional and spiritual well-being. I want to encourage you to build a system that prevents leaders from being burned out within your organization/church with the checkpoints listed above. It starts with continuous preventative maintenance. Our churches today are making the mistake of getting involved much too late. Many times we won't reach out until after someone has crashed. We must put the resources and accountability in place to prevent burnout long before it happens. We desire for you and your team to have longevity in ministry and become the healthy leader that God desires for you to be.

It Ain't Rocket Surgery

Chapter 8

The Ministry Mechanics

Yes, we know there is no such thing as Rocket Surgery. But, isn't it true that the church can make even the simplest of things difficult? Organizations always drift toward complexity. We are really good at taking things that are supposed to be simple and making them complicated. We make choosing a paint color for our church building incredibly difficult with layers of committees and votes. We can make walking with Jesus complicated by creating rules and lists that aren't even in the Bible.

This isn't anything new. In fact Jesus saw much of the same thing during His time on earth. Jesus was teaching and preaching everywhere He went. He came up on a group of Pharisees (which could be likened to some church leadership today) and they tried to test His knowledge. Matthew 22:34-36 shares the story:

...the Pharisees got together. One of them, an expert in the law, tested him with this question: "Teacher, which is the greatest commandment in the Law?"

Jesus replied: "'Love the Lord your God with all your heart and with all your soul and with all your mind.' This is the first and greatest commandment. And the second is like it: 'Love your neighbor as yourself. All the Law and the Prophets hang on these two commandments."

At the time there were 613 laws (six hundred thirteen!) that "good followers of God" were supposed to adhere to. The leaders spent hours and hours debating which laws were most important. Jesus came in and basically said "It's time to rethink this whole thing...Love God and Love People." Everything else will follow if you get these two right! Things had become so complicated and Jesus showed up and simplified the process.

We tend to complicate life and ministry with things that really do not matter. Ever find yourself doing something and wonder "How on earth did I end up here?" You're not alone. We meet pastors and leaders every single week who are alone, dejected, and overwhelmed by the tasks in front of them.

How do we break the cycle? How do we go the other direction? Here are a few areas where you can make simple adjustments that will produce results.

Clean is Free

Remember those Febreze commercials a while back about being nose blind? The general idea was that when you are in a room that smells bad for any length of time, you don't notice the odor. However, when a new person walks into the room, it's really evident to the new person that there is a big odor. Febreze wanted to put an end to "nose-blind" situations and help you eliminate embarrassing smells in your house that you may not even smell.

The Ministry Mechanics do Weekend Service Evaluations at churches across the country every month. The single issue that pops up more than anything else is cleanliness. There is a strong correlation between clean churches being growing churches and not-so-clean churches plateauing or even declining. These pastors come to us dejected about the lack of momentum and movement. We point to the stuff piled up around the buildings that they've gone "nose blind" to so they can see it. After so long, it's hard for you to look at your own building, staff, and organization with fresh eyes. That's why its so great to get an objective third party to give feedback and constructive criticism.

We learned this concept from watching organizations like Starbucks and Life.Church. They teach their teams to understand the expectations and standards for their stores/churches and challenge their people to be proactive in addressing situations regularly that are out of line with their vision. Starbucks refers to them as "Value Walks." Everyday their leaders take value walks around their stores to ensure that the location is meeting or exceeding the expectations set by the organization and leaders.

Things that you may be nose blind to sometimes can be so obvious as a table or even a small extension cord that is left in a common area for weeks at a time. While those are simple and clean examples, we've seen even worse situations where safety and security are at great risk because no one is in charge of ensuring that things are clean and ready to go. Keeping a building clean and organized seems like a no brainer to us, in our weekend service evaluations, we found that cleanliness is not always well done and is usually low on the priority list for many churches and pastors.

Leaders really need to train their eyes and mind to have an attention to these kinds of details. We were recently having lunch at a national burrito chain when we noticed a sign advertising their Christmas specials. This was normally a good thing except for the fact that it was March. Three months after Christmas was over, they had gone nose blind to the sign and the fact it was out of date! Get out and walk around. Change your perspective. Take some values walks around your property and with your team. It will be an eye-opening experience.

If you want to grow your church or organization, the first place to start is with the cleanliness question. Is it presentable? Is it clean? Does everything have a place? If not, what are you waiting for? Clean is free and it will go a long way toward building credibility, establishing trust, and making a significant connection with your guests. It ain't rocket surgery, keep the building clean…It's free!

Indicators Your Church is Over-Programmed

Several years ago I (Jeremy) was speaking at a church of around 250 meeting in a sanctuary that held around 500. The church had plateaued in previous years and was searching for their identity. Before the service I was walking in the lobby area and there was an old school bulletin board with what seemed like 200 programs on the wall. To me it seemed like they literally had a program for nearly every person that attended the church. I asked the pastor if he really had that many programs and he said "no, but if people have that need, we will fill it." It was certainly a noble gesture but it was backwards thinking and a miserable attempt to be all things to all people. It was a vision that lacked clarity and a ship without a clear direction. The church had not established a set of values as a filter for programming decisions.

Still to this day, there is an addiction in the church and it's not what you think. We have an addiction to starting new things without a proper understanding of exactly why and how it fits into the vision of the church. We are becoming deluged with an exorbitant amount of programs that were once great for a season but serve no purpose today and are failing. We have fooled ourselves into thinking more is better. More isn't always better, especially if it isn't done well. You could fill up a website with ministries but if they aren't reaching anyone or impacting lives then what's the point? Don't be ok with programs that have phased into mediocrity or even obscurity. Find a need in your community and be the church that meets that need. Every church and every leader has to get an understanding of the culture and people you live and work with to know how to best reach people. If you try to be all things to all people, you end up pleasing no one.

We can brag about our giant list of things that we do without giving the purpose for why we do things. The sad thing is that we sometimes don't realize what we are doing because it's all that we knew growing up. We just thought you needed a young adult Sunday school class and didn't realize that young adults don't want to get up early for Sunday school. We believed that we needed scrapbooking class for senior adults because it's always been that way. Unfortunately the phrase that kills many churches today is: "WE'VE ALWAYS DONE IT THAT WAY." If you want to keep failing, continue to do the same things because it's always done that way. Evaluate the programs that you have in your church and decide which ones still fit the vision of the church and which ones should be put to rest. When was the last time you knew something was dead and then you had the courage to kill it. If the answer is never, it may be time to rethink the vision for your programming. It ain't rocket surgery. Don't try to do it all. Find your thing and be good at it. Be a church that is known for being awesome at something. What does your community need that "something" to be?

Maybe you don't know if your church is over-programmed or not. Here are 5 indicators that your church has way too many programs.

1. You Have an Exhaustive List of Programs

If you are constantly updating your master list of programs and you have hired someone to keep up with this list, you might be over-programmed. If it's really that hard to keep up with, then it's time to trim the list and evaluate which ones need to stay and which one need to go. At times it can be like the popular yet mildly disturbing TV show, "Hoarders." You get sentimentally attached to a program and you can't get rid of it. So you tuck it away in the church basement just to keep yourself or someone else happy. This never works. What once was really helpful and had purpose, now doesn't have a demand.

2. You Struggle to Find Leaders for Programs

We hear this all the time: the struggle to find qualified leaders is real. Instead of pulling teeth to find a leader for a non-essential ministry, ask yourself the hard question. Why are we still doing this? If you can't find a leader for that struggling ministry, then is it possible that no one is interested in this ministry. It shouldn't be that difficult. Remember if it's striking a chord with your church, there will be a line of people ready to lead that vibrant ministry.

3. You Have the Same People Leading Multiple Programs

While it's great to have people who are diverse in their skill set and have the capacity for two ministries, it's not always a good idea. Many times eager leaders are willing to put more on their plate for the sake of the Kingdom or for the sake of the church. There are also those who will do anything the pastor asks of them. The problem with that is that that eager individual will be burned out in a year because they didn't do the thing that drives their passion. Instead they filled the role because no one else would. You have to love the heart of someone that is willing to take on more; however, you must ask yourself if this is the most beneficial position to put that volunteer in. Many times the answer is no, because it doesn't fix the bigger problem of why no one else will volunteer for that role. In the short term, it seems like a genius idea, but you need to preserve that rock star volunteer for the long haul and help that volunteer determine where they are most passionate to serve.

4. Your Team Doesn't Know A Program Existed

I have actually been in staff meetings of larger churches and experienced this myself. A fellow staff member talked about an internal ministry that I didn't know we had at the church. Even though it was a valid ministry and seemed to be a good idea, it hadn't gotten any traction since its inception. When this happens, maybe it's time to stop holding onto our nostalgic ministries that no one knows about. If a tree falls in the forest....You get my point.

5. If you Allow Anyone with A Burden to Start a Program

This is a difficult one. I will admit that I have been in this situation many times. The heart of the person is golden, however it doesn't always fit through the filter of the vision of the church. That doesn't mean that you won't pray for this ministry and be their cheerleader, it just simply means that it doesn't have to be a church program. Just because it doesn't fit the church and doesn't have a church label doesn't mean it doesn't meet the needs of someone and it doesn't mean that it's not a worthwhile or valid ministry opportunity. Instead of rejection, come from the position of releasing that person to start a ministry or even a non-profit. Many times people are waiting on our permission. If someone is upset that the church won't adopt their idea, then their motive for the idea is wrong. A person that has a sincere passion, will not be concerned about its affiliation or label. Send them in the right direction to fulfill their vision and it becomes a win for them and for the church.

The Importance of Values

"You won't do ministry that really matters until you define what really matters." - Aubrey Malphurs

When we started The Ministry Mechanics, we knew we wanted to have clearly defined core values. Values that would be a filter for everything we did. We both had worked at churches and organizations that had clearly defined values and everything they did flowed through these pillars. Adversely we had also worked in churches/organizations that didn't have their core values defined, in fact they didn't even see the need for these values. What we discovered was that the organizations that did have them defined, knew exactly who they were and generally ran smoothly. The organizations that didn't see the need tended to fly by the seat of their pants and was prone to change course every time there was a strong downwind. At times they were paralyzed by indecision because they didn't know who they were and it seemed like they were prepping for Rocket Surgery. Walt Disney's brother, Roy E. Disney once said, "It's Not hard to make decisions once you know what your values are." Disney is a place that makes decisions based on the values that matter to them and they never move away from those values.

As a ministry we always want to know exactly who we are and what we stand for and if times ever get tough, we will stay strong in the foundation we have established. We want to always protect those core values and make decisions based on them. If we ever have an idea or something new that we want to add we would run it through the filter of our values to see if it fits who we are. Those values are simply Give, Inspire, Grow and Multiply. There is nothing magical about these four values, but they are ours. It doesn't have to be complicated. It simplifies anything we choose to do. You must discover what values define who you are and begin to make decisions based on that discovery.

Ten Thousand Little Things

While we tend to overcomplicate things by trying to perform rocket surgery, there is also not a quick fix. When we've worked at churches that are growing and healthy, we would get tons of guests and the first thing people want to know is "How did you do it?" This question was always looking for the silver bullet or the magic bean of an answer that will transform their church or organization into a big movement overnight. The truth is that it's not any one thing. It's ten thousand little decisions that make the difference. Overnight success stories simply aren't the norm and usually aren't overnight. They are usually years into it and then they explode for 10,000 little reasons. While there are instances where churches and organizations grow incredibly quickly, that isn't typical.

The best place to start in building momentum and reaching people is systematically changing little things over time. We encourage pastors and leaders to focus on the things that matter. Hard work and attention to detail really go a long way toward building a successful organization. As you start working on the little things, they start to snowball and build momentum. What would happen if every week you made one simple adjustment in your organization? What would happen if every week you made a subtle shift toward doing things with excellence? In 5 years, you wouldn't even recognize your organization. It's the little things that will determine the difference between success and failure for leaders. Neglecting to do the little things will keep you from getting close to the big things that God wants you to do.

The key is to enjoy the process, identify the things that are important to you, stop doing the things that aren't important, and work hard! Remind yourself, this ain't rocket surgery.

PEOPLE ARE PIVOTAL

CHAPTER 9

THE MINISTRY MECHANICS

We recently checked into a hotel and the girl at the front desk didn't have on a name badge. We asked her name and she told us it was Haley. She added that we weren't going to find her name anywhere in the building because she didn't want anyone saying anything bad about her. Leading people isn't for the faint of heart. It's difficult for sure. I've heard the phrase "Leadership is lonely" so many times. While it's true that being a leader will force you to make a hard decision or deal with a difficult customer or church member from time to time, we wholeheartedly believe that being a lonely leader is a choice. The quote should read something like this instead: "Leadership is lonely but you never have to do it alone." Have you ever felt alone? Like really alone? Not like "I got a night to myself alone" but like "Oh man, it's all on me!" alone. It's a scary feeling. Even scarier is when things don't work out and it's all on you. You're standing on an island and everyone is looking at you wondering how you could let this happen.

"Leaders must avoid isolation, insulation and idolization. Instead pursue accountability, community, humility and self awareness." - Brad Lomenick

We really value strong leadership. It's one of the biggest things that sets successful organizations apart from mediocre ones. It takes great leaders to accomplish big goals. That being said, ministry is not an environment for lone wolves. There is no such thing as a one man wolf pack! Much more can be accomplished in a pack. You can't do this alone and besides it's way more fun when you do it together. The victories are sweeter, those God moments are more memorable because you have others there that can remember those moments during the times it gets tough. The best leaders celebrate as a team and accept the loss as an individual. It takes great courage to lead with that kind of vision, but in the end, you and your organization will reap the benefits of this kind of leadership.

Building these types of relationships and connections is the best way to fight off moral failure. By having real relationships and opening your life to those around you, you will find it easy to be real and authentic. We need to take pastors off of pedestals and down to the streets where the people are living, where they can be most useful and effective. God doesn't want a perfect pastor, he wants an available and authentic pastor. God doesn't need another Billy Graham or Andy Stanley, he already has one of each of those guys. God wants us to be a broken vessel that He can use over and over again. I want Him to remind me daily of my desperate need for more of Him and much less of me in my life.

Character Counts

During the lowest point of my life, I (Jeremy) knew I needed strong people to lean on and to stand beside in ministry. Even though I didn't have a moral failure, I needed to be restored spiritually, emotionally and in every other possible way. I assembled a tremendous team of six Godly men to surround me with prayer, accountability and friendship. These men were strong and grounded in their faith, a majority were fellow pastors. These were the right people with the same vision and values I had for my life. Accountability is so vital in ministry. My personal board of directors kept me in check during my restoration process. I really regret that I didn't have this type of accountability in my life prior to hitting rock bottom.

We've all worked for leaders who seem to isolate and insulate themselves from the outside world. When this happens they lose the transparency needed to lead and then they begin to lose credibility. We unfortunately live in a culture that honors charisma over character. They may be able to fool people for a while, but it never lasts. Not only is it dangerous, they lose effectiveness and become disconnected from the team. They are unavailable, many times not present and have no interest in changing. They fail to realize that ministry is meant to be done together. These leaders are usually the first ones to complain that they feel like they have no friends and are completely alone. It's them against the world. As your church or organization grows, there will certainly be temptation to fall into that trap. You may think that it's easier to do it yourself or it's easier to just figure it out on your own. In the short term, that may be true, but to share the leadership is going to take involving others in the journey. The best leaders remain engaged, are aware of what's happening in their organization, and show that they care about the people they are serving with.

Mark 1:16-20 shows us how to build a team:

"As Jesus walked beside the Sea of Galilee, he saw Simon and his brother Andrew casting a net into the lake, for they were fishermen. "Come, follow me," Jesus said, "and I will send you out to fish for people." At once they left their nets and followed him.

"When he had gone a little farther, he saw James son of Zebedee and his brother John in a boat, preparing their nets. Without delay he called them, and they left their father Zebedee in the boat with the hired men and followed him."

Even Jesus knew He couldn't do it alone. Everywhere He went, He was finding people to invite to join their movement. He wasn't looking for the best resumes from churchstaffing.com. He didn't need to check their LinkedIn profile. He found some humble fishermen and called them by name and asked them to follow along for the journey. How many people in your church or organization are just sitting by, waiting for someone to pour into them or to invite them to leave their nets behind?

Every time we walk into a church, I always look for the most underutilized talent in the building. I can spot them a mile away. People that have been forgotten because they grew up in the church, they've been around forever, they don't have the pedigree, or they don't look like me. Don't just accumulate an organization full of followers. Spend your life building an army of leaders that will carry out your vision and find their own in the process.

What about you? Who believed in you? Who invited you along for the journey when you probably didn't deserve it? Who poured into you? Chris and I have been blessed by incredible mentors and leaders who have poured into our lives with no expectation of anything in return. We've both been equally blessed to mentor and develop leaders who are now located all over the world, making a difference in the lives of others. Believing in someone changes their perspective and activates something inside of them that proves that they can accomplish anything. Many times believing in someone gives them the courage to step out into the unknown. It empowers them to lead and when that happens it not only benefits the individual but the entire organization. Best of all, you will eliminate personal isolation, grow as a leader, and build influence. You will still have to lead, but you don't have to do it alone.

The Right Fit

If you want to go fast, go by yourself, if you want to go far, put the right people in place and go together. One of the biggest roadblocks of progress is putting the wrong people on your team. Jim Collins talks about this in his book, *Good to Great*. In the book he looks at why some companies make the leap and why some don't. He talks about putting the right people on the bus.

I have seen churches and organizations put the wrong people on their team and the lasting negative impact that it has on others and the organization as a whole. It even has the potential to derail the whole thing which could take years to recover. I have seen churches close their doors because of a bad hire or believing in the wrong people. The stakes are too high to entrust responsibility to the wrong person. Will we always get it right? No, because everyone is human and we don't always know what we are getting with people. At times the people that seem perfect just don't work out. The ones who are on the borderline and we may doubt suddenly become our greatest team members.

We talked in the last chapter about the importance of values in any organization. One of the ways to discover the right people that might fit your organization is to use the filter of your values. Normally the ones that best fit your team are the ones who fit the values that matter the most to you. The things that are important to you will also be the things that are important to them. Your passion will match their passion. When you hire based on your values, you will see your team unify and become one as you chase the common goals that you have set.

Ultimately, you must have strong faith that God will put the right people in your path. That He will send the perfectly imperfect person to become part of your story and in turn you will become part of theirs. Trust God to assemble the right team with the right character and passion that will be wired to come alongside you in the mission.

Taking Care of People

How do you connect and relate to your team? As leaders we like to think big! We like to blow it out and hit a home run with every event we do. When it comes to developing leaders, it's often the simplest things that have the biggest impact. Everyone likes to talk about themselves. Everyone likes to share their passion. When was the last time you sat face-to-face to listen to your team members talk about their work? When was the last time you heard about the impact that your staff is making in your organization and beyond?

You will experience one of the biggest leadership shifts in your ministry by simply sitting down for lunch with departments to learn names, swap stories, and listen. It doesn't take much. People just want to feel needed and known. This kind of leadership will require you to be vulnerable and let down your guard. But that sliver of vulnerability will be where the greatest growth will occur in you and your organization.

You may be saying, "I don't have time to invest in others." Let me remind you, as a leader that is *the* most important thing that you do. That's it, that's the line of work you are in, the people business. If you are too busy to invest in others, then you are filling your days with things that are far less important than impacting people for Christ and developing them to be the leader that God is calling them to be. How selfish would it be if you kept everything you have learned from other reliable people and you didn't pass it on to someone else? It would be a shame and more importantly it's blatant disobedience.

When I (Chris) was first getting started in ministry, my boss invited me over on a Saturday morning to wash my car with him while he washed his. We got to talk about anything and everything. It was so awesome. I remember thinking "We should totally do this every week!" He would go on to call this concept The Ministry Of Presence. While I've seen lots of books and articles about the topic, I saw firsthand the power of simply spending time with another person. No app, podcast, or seminar can replace good, ol' fashioned connection with someone on your team.

You have the potential to completely change the trajectory of someone's life by just saying yes to investing in them. Maybe that person that you are supposed to invest in doesn't even know their capabilities. You hold the power to speak truth into their life, build them up and pour everything that you have into them. Who knows the impact that you could have on someone's life just by being obedient.

The same is true when you have children. From the moment they are born, there is a plan for growth and development. As parents you work with them when it comes to crawling and then the process of taking their first steps. Without your guidance, the child would fall flat on his face every time and wouldn't even know where to start. Because of your investment in your child, they can succeed in life. As a parent you are the greatest influencer in their life and it's up to you to develop them.

In the business world you will frequently hear the term "return on investment" or ROI. The goal is to get a financial return that exceeds the amount of your investment to make a profit. In the ministry world the greatest commodity you can invest in is people and the ROI is defined very differently. In fact the greatest return on your investment into people is a Kingdom return that can't truly be measured in this life.

You may think that this is a consumeristic way of looking at things and that couldn't be further from the truth. The only profit that we are reaping is building the Kingdom of God. In the church today, we immediately rush to judgement when anyone talks about numbers. I don't know how many times I have heard someone complaining about a church that cares about numbers. Numbers simply represent lives changed, souls won for the Kingdom and every story of life change matters to God. He found it so significant that all throughout scripture specific numbers are mentioned. 5000 were fed, 3000 came to know God and many more. Someone was counting back then and I'm sure there were those who gave them flack over the counting and they were probably accused of being all about the numbers.

Numbers are significant to God and they should be significant to us. As you are obedient, the numbers will happen. It starts with investing in one life. Paul challenges us all in 2 Timothy 2:2 to invest in others and that pattern of pouring into other people continues:
"You have heard me teach things that have been confirmed by many reliable witnesses. Now teach these truths to other trustworthy people who will be able to pass them on to others."

This is not only the essence of sharing the Gospel but also developing other leaders. The investment that you make by teaching and developing others is not just temporary, it's eternal and contagious. Developing leaders and passing it on to others begins with one and it spreads to many. This develops a culture of investing in others and allows growth to happen. When this type of investment culture isn't designed properly, then an organization's growth is stunted and you become stagnant.

This is why you see many churches stay small, there is limited discipleship happening, and there is no intentional plan to develop leaders. What would happen if you built that type of culture in your church or organization? You would see a momentum and a new vibrant soul in your church. Instead of you doing every single thing within your church, you begin to develop leaders to grow up and serve alongside you with people who are truly wired to do certain things that maybe you aren't wired to do. There is nothing more special than developing leaders and releasing them into ministry. Make people a priority and watch them grow.

GRAB THE LAWNMOWER

CHAPTER 10

THE MINISTRY MECHANICS

The first real job I (Chris) had as kid was mowing my neighbor's yard. For forty dollars, I'd hop on his mower, drop it into gear, lower the blade, and make some cold, hard cash. It was almost therapeutic. I loved being on that mower. I felt independence and a sense of accomplishment. I saved every check that summer and paid for my first guitar. Needless to say, all these years later, I still love to mow.

A couple years back, I had some folks come up to me after a service to share about a big mowing project. The couple shared that they had a neighbor who had grass that was overgrown and a yard that was completely out of control. Their suggestion was to have the church send a team of people out to their neighborhood and knock out this mission project. At first, I was going to encourage them to put it on our list and then God zapped me and nudged me to offer some encouragement. I simply asked the question: "Do you all own a mower?" They looked at me with a puzzled look and said, "Yes." I then dropped a truth bomb and said, "I think God may be asking you to do it." The husband got a grin and said "It never occurred to me to just go do it!" These folks felt like they needed to ask permission to go out and do the very thing that God wanted them to do...serve! It was at that moment, I realized it was time to rethink the way we did missions ministry.

God loves it when we are faithful in the small things. He loves to see that He can trust us to manage and handle the task at hand for that season. When we prove our faithfulness, He entrusts us with more and more. Luke 16:10 says, *"Whoever can be trusted with very little can also be trusted with much..."* As any organization grows, it gets increasingly difficult to continue to excel. Good organizations and leadership adapt and adjust programming to be scalable and reproducible. If they don't, managing the ministry can become taxing and expensive. A few chapters back, we encouraged you to de-program, to decide what programs God has called you to complete. This chapter is about de-centralizing, taking off the controls to unleash explosive growth in you, your team, and your organization.

The Program

Once we started looking into the way we ran the missions program, we realized there were a lot of resources that were disappearing because of an inefficient process and too much institutional control. For some context, when our church started, we did monthly mission projects and the turnout was fantastic. Groups would descend on a local mission organization and pour out love and support, which was the goal. But, as the church grew to over ten thousand in attendance, we kept adding project after project to keep up with demand. We would have needed to hire 10 full-time staffers to provide enough mission projects at all our locations. Also, as our organization grew in attendance, policies started entering the picture. Now, we had to plan forty to fifty projects a year AND provide transportation to satisfy insurance requirements. We were spending tens of thousands a year just to drive our folks to and from projects and we found that the same three hundred people (at a ten thousand plus member church) were the ones serving on all the projects. As soon as we would announce a project, it would instantly fill up with the same ol' people. The program would only be as good as our ability to create and manage projects. We began to realize that the only way people were going to be involved in serving is if we organized it for them. That wasn't the way God intended it to be. We needed people to change their thinking from missions being an event we go to and start seeing it as a way of life. Everyone in our church living on mission, everyday!

We knew we needed to blow up the model and start over. Our goal then became to engage more people from our church in serving on mission projects. We went to the drawing board to dream up a model that could handle a limitless amount of people serving. That's where 50 States of Summer was born. We rolled it out in a big way. We announced the idea on social media live from Times Square in New York while we were attending a meeting with a missions organization in the Big Apple. It blew up and tons of people tuned in for the announcement and got excited about it.

We set out with a goal to have people from our church serve in all 50 states during that summer. It was a simple process:

1. Decide as a family to tag a portion of your summer vacation and give it away and serve wherever you go.
2. Visit our "Travel Agents" in the lobby and pick up a "Travel Guide." The guide contained lists of local and national organizations that you could schedule an appointment to serve with, or just choose your own. There were coloring sheets for the trip for the kids and stickers for your luggage.
3. Snap a picture with our live mascot "Roadie" (he was in the shape of the US) and get everyone talking about the projects before you go.
4. Serve on your trip.
5. Snap a picture of you holding a card in the shape of our church logo and use the hashtag #50StatesOfSummer on all your social media.
6. Share your story with us. We believe in the power of stories and this encouraged others to serve as they traveled during the summer. We underestimated the impact that it would have in all fifty states.

The stories started rolling in and one by one, states started coming off the board. We had giant maps at each location with peel off stickers to mark each new state that was covered. In 12 weeks we had over 700 people serve in 50 states and 11 countries. We had people taking trips just to help us knock out our last couple of states. It was incredible. So many stories of serving others and being Jesus to a dying world. It also generated momentum when people returned from vacation and got them excited about serving where they were planted in their own community. We witnessed so many wins. We doubled the number of people serving in 12 weeks because we took ourselves out of the equation. They no longer needed permission from the church staff to serve. We decentralized the concept of serving and put the decision-making back in the hands of our people. Once, a story would come in, we'd celebrate.

We'd mark it on the maps, go crazy on social media, and celebrate in our services.

The best news of all is that we doubled our participation for one third the cost of transporting our people to and from our projects the previous year. It was incredible.

Now this is just one example, but how do you need to make some adjustments to your processes to get some big wins in your church? How can you engage more volunteers to serve? How can you equip more people to lead small groups? How can you get more people excited about the vision and mission of your church? More importantly, how can you get your people to start living out their own personal calling instead of asking you for permission?
How can you do it? That simple question I asked our volunteers: "Is God calling you to do it?" and see what happens. Just because someone comes to you with an idea, doesn't necessarily mean it's for you to do. It may be that they need confirmation, encouragement, and a push to do it themselves. When they have their aha moment and complete the project on their own, celebrate like crazy.

The People

One thing that really brought home this win was all the amazing things we heard from the stories of serving. We learned about new ministries to partner with in our community and some people found their calling through the project. There were guys and gals in our church literally running huge non-profits and missions organizations we didn't even know about. Now we did, and we were able to point people with similar passions to their organizations. The old process was gone and now we had a new strategy to get more people involved than ever before. Stories of changed lives always point back to the most important and powerful tool your organization has: people.

What would happen if you started empowering people to become the hands and feet of Jesus? What could happen if people started grabbing the lawn mower and serving with passion and intensity? What momentum have you missed from trying to manage or program the spiritual life of the folks in your church? Do you believe it's possible to empower your team members and unleash a movement of God in your church or organization? Of course it is! By developing leaders and releasing people into their passion, you can bring change to your church and your community. What are the characteristics of these kinds of leaders? We get this question often. For us it boils down to four traits:

1. Support

We certainly don't want to surround ourselves with "yes" people, but it sure is nice to have a team of people that are committed to the mission, vision, and values of the leader and the organization. Team members should be supportive and generally excited about the direction of the organization. It shouldn't be a struggle, it should be natural. Great leaders need to support the team and the organization with their:

  a. Talk - Words matter. The way we speak with or respond to people speaking to us is so critical. Great team members support with the way they talk. It's should be positive in nature and clear in communication. The Book of James warns us of the danger of a tongue that is out of control. Don't allow your words to become gasoline to the fires of bitterness or condescension or negativity. Use words to provide life-giving waters of encouragement, motivation and grace.

  b. Time - Be present. It's hard to say you're a part of a team if you're never working hard at practice or suited up for the games. Great team members are around more than they aren't. Hebrews reminds us of the importance of gathering together. Your presence will be an encouragement to someone else. The average person attends church less that 50% of the time. That's twenty six weeks out of the year. That's the minimum. Don't let the minimum be your legacy. Get your uniform on and get in the game.

c. Talent - Skills to spare. Everyone has some kind of gift to share with the world. Don't keep it to yourself. Cross that line from being a taker to being a giver. What do you like to do? What are your passions? What are your skills? Find the place where the needs of your organization or church intersect with your abilities and put them to work. There's no better way to support your organization and leaders than with using the gifts that God has uniquely given you!

d. Treasure - Live generously. The Bible talks about money more than any other topic. It's a huge part of our everyday lives. Use the resources you have to bless others. This is usually the last means of support to show up in the life of a leader. It's also the first to go when leaders lose focus on supporting the organization. Don't be that person. Give and live generously. God loves it when we give cheerfully. Show support to your organization and leaders by giving and living generously.

2. Missional

The best leaders are intentional in every area of their lives. From the parking lot, to the front door, to the chairs, to the service, and back again, they live with a clear mission. Most churches have some version of The Great Commission as their mission. "Love God, Love Others" is the concept. This begins with a selfless attitude and an others-first mentality. Sometimes we overcomplicate what it means to live "on mission." Even the simplest gestures can have a HUGE impact!

I (Chris) have a confession to make. I like old-school music. Glen Campbell is a legend, okay. I don't do a lot of Justin Bieber in my car. It's not my thing. Not only do I prefer the classics on my car stereo, but in church. I've worked at and even led modern worship at some incredibly progressive churches. That being said, I like the old stuff. BUT...I know that newer music and a relevant sound goes a long way toward reaching a younger generation of worshippers. What I found is that by putting my preference aside, I could reach and lead more people to Jesus! That's a trade I'll take

EVERY SINGLE TIME! Jesus came to seek and save that which was lost…not make sure Chris enjoys the service.

We are big believers in the idea that mature, seasoned, and supportive Christians need to give up some of the things we love for things we love even more. Supportive leaders are willing to get out of their comfort zone and do anything they can to help others know Jesus. When your pastor asks you to attend a different service, park far away, sit up front, or serve, it's not to make you miserable. No, it's to help you see the mission behind every single one of those decisions. When you see that attending an early or late service opens up a seat for new people to easily find a seat in the service, it becomes a mission and not an inconvenience. When you see that parking far away allows someone new to get into the building easily, it becomes a mission and not an inconvenience. When you give up your seat so a new family can sit together, it becomes a mission and not an inconvenience. When you keep the bathrooms clean and stocked or hold babies during the service, it becomes a mission and not an inconvenience.

3. Servanthood

It's so rare to find a leader who is willing to do the hard things and stay to the end. Be a finisher. Don't let anything stop you from serving and getting your hands dirty. It's not glamorous, but God LOVES it when we serve. In fact, I'd say we're modeling Christ most when we serve others. He was so faithful to serve the world by staying the course and dying on the cross for each of us. When we serve, we pick up the cross and bear the burdens of others.

When I (Chris) was interning at my first church, I loved going to lunch with the Facilities Director at our church. He cracked me up and become a great mentor and friend (and still is to this day). After lunch out one day, we stopped in the restroom before we left. As we were wrapping up washing our hands, I noticed he took paper towels and wiped down the entire counter around the sink before we left. I was totally thrown off by this. What on earth would make a person want to do something like that? I had to ask!

His words still resonate today: "leave things better than you found them."

That was a dagger to the heart. He modeled servanthood in some incredible ways. Not only was the counter at the restaurant clean, my heart was changed also! 20 years later, I'm sharing that story with you. Serving is a great way to model the kind of behavior and effort you want from your team. If you want people around you that serves others, it begins with you. Lead the way and watch the culture around you change.

4. Aware

The Holy Spirit is the best guide in the world for leaders. Connecting to God's word, a consistent prayer life, and the power of the Holy Spirit is critical for Godly leaders. You have to keep your heart in the right place to sense the guiding of the Spirit of God. When you connect to God on this level, it helps you become aware of others, of opportunities, and of moments. Great leaders sense when the timing is right to share the gospel with co-workers, family, and friends. Great leaders know when God is leading them to charge after a dream and when it's time to slow their pace to explain the vision and take time to develop others. Great leaders can feel the momentum and are not afraid of the moment. Instead of shrinking by the weight of the situations they find themselves in, they lead with strength and courage because they are prayed up and ready to do whatever God calls them to!

The Right People In The Right Place

Your church doesn't have to do everything for everyone. Feel the freedom to find organizations that are doing it well, and partner with them. You will feel some pressure during the change, but the loss of effectiveness will be temporary. Over time, the results will follow and your church or organization will be positioned to grow and scale like never before. Sometimes, the fact that our programs and processes aren't built for growth will be the very thing that causes people to disappear. If they can't find a place to connect or get involved, they slip away and go to the next place or no place at all. By making some subtle adjustments, you can experience sustained growth. Not only will this kind of change bring excellence and strategic partnerships to the forefront, it will get your church or organization involved in the community. When leaders find their calling and a place to fulfill it, amazing things happen! It's time to tell some people to grab their lawn mower and get to work serving in their church and community.

I (Chris) found the couple that came to me about mowing their neighbors grass and I asked them how it went. They were overcome with joy and satisfaction that God had opened the door for them to serve their neighbors. They found out that a husband had recently passed away and the widow was unable to take care of it. From that day forward, the family included the widow's yard in their weekly lawn care routine. The entire family worked together to serve their neighbor, we celebrated with them, and their relationship with God became a tangible and personal thing… not an event to attend.

You're Doing It Wrong

Chapter II

The Ministry Mechanics

This chapter isn't about worship style or theological preference. It isn't an arrogant statement that assumes that we know more than you. We are not saying that if you aren't doing it our way you are doing it wrong. We don't believe there is one way to do ministry. Every situation is different and is customizable to fit your community. We are simply saying if you are not having fun in ministry and you aren't being intentional about building a positive culture within your team, then yes you are doing it wrong. Will everything always be fun? No. Despite it not being Rocket Surgery, there will be times when it will be difficult. One thing is for sure, life is way too short to be miserable in ministry. We don't want you as the leader to be miserable. If you are a miserable leader, theres a good chance you are going to lead a miserable church, organization or team. Being miserable is a choice and we choose to drive away anything that would make us feel that way.

Throughout our time of working in churches, we've been the self proclaimed "Kings of Fun." Ministry shenanigans is our speciality because we don't know any other way. Of course we are talking about good clean fun. For example on Tuesdays, we would eat at the Johnny Carino's Italian restaurant in Houston. We mainly went there because of this amazing deal that they had at lunch. We both could get out of there for under five dollars a piece. Then they closed down because the deal was too good I suppose. Before they shut their doors, we were able to meet our friend Meredith. She was a bright young college student that worked there as a hostess. Any time we go out to eat, we try to encourage others and have fun with the people that work there. We bring our fun environment that we have created wherever we go. We realize that work isn't always easy so we take it upon ourselves to do whatever it takes to make their day brighter. Our goal is to make the server/employee feel like a million bucks when we walk out of the door.

On this particular day, we were talking to Meredith and we asked her where she went to church. Much to our surprise, she told us that she went to the church where we were working at the time, but she had been away at college. Her family had attended for quite some time. Up until this point Meredith had never served in the church. We asked her to become one of our 50 States of Summer travel agents, which volunteered to get people connected in serving. She said yes and she became a member of our team. We could've gone into the same restaurant every Tuesday, kept our head down, our mouths closed and never shared the joy that God had so freely poured into our lives. Instead we chose to express that joy and opened up our lives to others and because of that simple act of obedience, Meredith took her next step in her faith to serve others. All because two guys believed that it's always best to inject fun into anything we do.

To do that you must step away from the air conditioned office of comfort every once in a while. If you want to do real ministry you must choose to love others, break out of the building and go into the community. Build relationships with people who aren't like you and people who don't already attend your church. Gone are the days of the come as you are church, we need to be a go where they are church.

We are not the type of leaders that get locked behind the desk all day nor do we take a Rapunzel approach to ministry, where we are trapped in an ivory tower and lead from afar. As we said in Chapter 4, *"That Ain't Us."* We don't feel that's the way God intended for us to lead. We made a decision long ago that we were going to have fun and we were going to create an environment for others to have fun. We know there are certainly times to be serious but there are also times where you just have to lighten up and enjoy this blessed opportunity that you have in ministry. The great leaders know how to shift between those gears.

Think about what you get to do on a daily basis. You get to be an advocate for Christ and an agent for life change. You are able to have a conversation with someone today that could alter the course of their life. You could pray with someone that is accepting Christ. You could be planting a seed in someone's heart to hear about Jesus for the first time. He chose you to do these things, so why would you do it begrudgingly or as if you are miserable, gritting your teeth the whole way. Why would you choose to get bogged down by the minutia of ministry and allow it drain you of the joy of your calling?

"I've decided that there's nothing better to do than go ahead and have a good time and get the most we can out of life. That's it—eat, drink, and make the most of your job. It's God's gift." **Ecclesiastes 3:12-13 MSG**

This passage is found in Ecclesiastes following a long list of seasons that we will go through in our life. For everything there is a season, a season to cry and to laugh, a season to grieve and to dance, etc. When the author Solomon concludes the statement, he says at the end of the day there is nothing like being happy and enjoying ourselves as much as we can for as long as we can. In the chapter before, Solomon talks about how we should find satisfaction in our work. Each and every moment of joy in doing what we are wired to do is a gracious gift from God. What will you choose to do with this gift? Will you make the most of every moment in ministry or will you focus on the negative side of the grind? You may not have control over that but you do have control over your response to the negative side of your calling. The remedy is to continue to have fun doing the very thing that sets your soul ablaze and allow God to daily pour joy into your heart. When this happens, it will change your perspective of "work." It won't be work anymore and it won't be something you feel that you need to escape or dread.

The Mondays

Every Sunday night on social media, I can't help to notice the barrage of posts about the daunted thought of the upcoming week. When did people become so miserable with entering a new week? We have become a society that lives for the next weekend. We say things like, "is it Friday yet?" or "it's almost the weekend!" I have noticed that some people are now calling Thursdays, "Friday Jr." Which leads me to believe that most people in our society today, do not enjoy what they are doing Monday through Friday. It saddens me to see so many people unhappy. Some folks seemingly have a case of the Mondays everyday.

This isn't the way God designed for us to live. He has given each one of us a burning passion and has wired every single person with a purpose. I can assure you that your purpose isn't just to make it to the weekend. He wants you to do something that matters. If you aren't doing that and you are dreading going back to work on Monday, maybe you are not living out your purpose. If you are so unhappy that it makes you physically sick when you think about it or if you consider calling in sick every single Monday morning, then maybe it's time to discover or rediscover your purpose. Stop mailing it in and going through the motions. I understand the fact that sometimes you have to do some things that you don't enjoy, maybe even work jobs that you don't like to be able to do what you really love. I have been there and gone through those seasons. However you can't stay in the perpetual state of dread. The weight is too heavy to carry and it will eventually break under the pressure, which will make things even worse.

If this is you, you may need to set out on a new adventure of finding the sweet spot of life. In baseball, when a pitcher throws you a pitch and you hit it on the sweet spot, that means you hit it on the solid part of the bat. It doesn't get any better when the ball makes contact with that spot. Usually when that happens it will be a homer or at the very least an extremely hard hit ball. The same is true when you find the sweet spot of life and ministry, good things tend to happen. You are simply knocking it out of the park and homers are fun.

In ministry it's really easy to focus so much on the weekend. For most of us we have been taught to make Sunday excellent. Some even have the "Sunday is our Super Bowl" mentality. There are tremendous expectations to get that day right. By focusing so much on Sundays, we tend to lose focus on what happens during the week. What we fail to understand is that what we do during the week prepares us for the weekend. The sweet spot in ministry happens when you knock it out of the park on the weekend and you are filled with so much excitement that you can't wait to do it all over again starting on Monday.

You don't have to shake off the dreaded Mondays because you are wired to do what you are doing. When you are in the sweet spot, you don't sit at home on Sunday night thinking of ways to call in sick, instead you are thinking of ways to innovate and cultivate ideas that will reach more people. When you are working in a fun and creative environment, Monday becomes a catalyst for the week rather than an anchor to your existence. You and your team will be on top of their game, rather than discarding that day because it's a Monday. Ask yourself the question, "How passionate am I about Mondays?" Your answer should be able to dictate if you are in the sweet spot or not.

If You Build It, They Will Stay

Last year we took a tour of several thriving churches in the eastern United States. We were doing research on ways to revamp our missions ministry, which we talked about in the last chapter. While we were at one particular church meeting with their team, we couldn't help to notice this giant chalkboard in their conference room. It had a list of several short values but these weren't values for their entire church, they had separate values for the staff. It was a set of values that really mattered to them and something that they were intentional about establishing and protecting. Most thriving churches today understand the need to be architects of positive staff culture. You are either building culture or you are allowing it, you get to choose. You will have team culture either way, it will be positive or negative and you have more control over that than you think. You have to show the courage to drive that desired culture. A culture that wins. When your team succeeds the whole organization wins

We were in Gatlinburg recently finishing up this book. We ate at one of my favorite places there called The Peddler. It's an old school steakhouse with a salad bar, of course every restaurant should have a salad bar. That's another topic for another day. When you walk into the restaurant, they had something that I had never really seen in any other establishment. Each and every employee had their picture on the wall in individual frames and below their name was the year they started with the company. and I noticed that all of the servers had been working there for a long time, some over 25 years. I was talking to the general manager and I had to ask him about this outlier because most restaurants have a very high turnover. What made this place in the Smoky Mountains different? I thought his answer might be the pay or some other perk but that wasn't the case. He said "we have made an intentional effort to build a fun and safe environment for our people. Even though we are not related, we are family."

This statement is reflected in their success, in their product and in their proven track record. They are known for having great customer service and of course great food. When you make an intentional effort to build a fun and safe environment, you will become like family. You will also begin to see team unity and it will instill loyalty. People want to stay where they are having fun and where they are appreciated. If you are building this type of team culture, it will break down dissension and will prevent fractured relationships. You will begin to love the people you are working with. You won't be pals with everyone but statistics show that when you have a friend at work, it greatly affects retention. When the mission and culture throws you in the same direction, people stay together and they will be loyal.

"Culture trumps vision" say's church growth guru Sam Chand.

He goes on to say that, "Culture—not vision or strategy—is the most powerful factor in any organization. It determines the receptivity of staff and volunteers to new ideas, unleashes or dampens creativity, builds or erodes enthusiasm, and creates a sense of pride or deep discouragement about working or being involved there. Ultimately, the culture of an organization— particularly in churches and nonprofit organizations, but also in any organization—shapes individual morale, teamwork, effectiveness, and outcomes."

Vision is useless without having the right team to carry it out. When you have a positive staff/team culture, your people will be more receptive and more passionate toward your vision than ever before. When you build it the right way, your team will feel more appreciated and loved and they will run through walls with the team and for the team.

Culture Killers

Once you have established your team culture, you must be aware of certain culture killers that will try to hijack what you have worked so hard to build. This is when you must go into protection mode and fend off the things that seek to destroy your design. Some of these killers are more subtle than others, but are just as dangerous. Be aware of anything that may have the resemblance of the following. Whatever you do, don't let these things permeate your positive team culture:

Gossip

"Don't pass on malicious gossip." **Exodus 23:1**
This is a silent, behind-the-scenes killer. Every team member must be on guard and keep themselves in check on this one. What may seem like an innocent conversation could morph into a dangerous wildfire that is so difficult to contain once it has begun. The first hint of gossip should be squashed immediately before it lingers and becomes destructive.

Complaining

"Do everything without complaining and arguing." **Philippians 2:14**

This is something that bogs down progress and changes the morale of a group in a heartbeat. Complaining is contagious because it may start with one but soon there are others that take on the characteristics of the people that they are around the most. This is something that just blankets the organization with negativity and if not handled properly can be harmful to everyone.

Silos

"Any kingdom divided by civil war is doomed. A family splintered by feuding will fall apart." **Luke 11:17**

Many times there will be a team member or a segment of team members that begin to do their own thing and veer from the mission and vision. This causes division within the ranks and creates silos of factions within the culture. These silos seek to break down unity and they usually have their own vision and agenda. This can't be tolerated. It is simply selfishness and has to be addressed at first notice. Much like any family, we realize you are not going to agree on everything. This is when you get behind closed doors, become real and raw with each other and then move forward. You must come out from behind the closed door meeting with a united front and an identical message. Friction is many times what starts the fire, it can be healthy but it has to come to a conclusion at the end of the day.

The Fun Police

"Summing it all up, friends, I'd say you'll do best by filling your minds and meditating on things true, noble, reputable, authentic, compelling, gracious—the best, not the worst; the beautiful, not the ugly; things to praise, not things to curse. Put into practice what you learned from me, what you heard and saw and realized. Do that, and God, who makes everything work together, will work you into his most excellent harmonies." **Philippians 4:8-9**

These are folks who are looking for ways to stop your fun in ministry. You can usually spot negative Debbie Downers a mile away. We fully understand that everyone won't be just like the leader, but if you want a positive culture be intentional about putting positive people on your team. Is everyone wired to be the life of the party? Of course not, but hopefully you will find people that will at the very least have fun in their own way in ministry. Negative people are like Hoover vacuum cleaners- they suck the positivity right out of the room. Beware of the Hoovers in ministry.

Blaming Others

"You, therefore, have no excuse, you who pass judgment on someone else, for at whatever point you judge another, you are condemning yourself, because you who pass judgment do the same things." **Romans 2:1**

There will be times where you or someone around you will drop the ball. You get to choose how to respond when this takes place and how you fix it. Will you pass the blame to someone else or will you accept it as yours? When you refuse to take ownership for your actions and shift blame to others, hard feelings will follow. At times this will be a major ripple in your team dynamic. This could easily be prevented by choosing to humble yourself and simply own your mistakes.

No matter the threat on the culture that you have built, you must put safeguards in place to fend off the enemy. Protecting the values and the team is of the utmost importance and can never be taken lightly. Always be on guard and ready when the threat comes because it will come sooner or later. Your preparation will determine the amount of damage that you will incur. The more prepared you are for the culture killers, the more likely you will be positioned properly to defend your values and will be able to minimize damage.

Building and protecting a positive and fun culture within your staff/team can make or break your organization. Ask yourself today what are the values that are important to your staff/team? When you discover what they are, write them down and post them everywhere you can. Instill in your team these values and stick with them, don't waver. By doing this, you are making an intentional effort to build culture within your organization. When you build the team culture, it makes it easier to build your church's culture as a whole. If you build it, they will stay!

BUILD THE CHURCH

CHAPTER 12

THE MINISTRY MECHANICS

"And now I'm going to tell you who you are, really are. You are Peter, a rock. This is the rock on which I will put together my church, a church so expansive with energy that not even the gates of hell will be able to keep it out." **Matthew 16:18 MSG**

God promises with absolute authority: *I will build my church.* He not only promised to build His church, but it will be a church that is so dynamic that not even the gates of hell could stop it. A church with tremendous depth, energy and momentum. This church that He loves so deeply is not a building. It's a people, with or without a building. A people so powerful that it has changed the world over the last 2000 plus years and will continue to do so until the end of time.

One part of our mission as The Ministry Mechanics is to simply "Build the Church." We are fully aware that it is God that will build His church. We want to come alongside His mission and be a part of something extraordinarily special. Christ died for the church, this beautiful bride that we still are a part of today. He believed so much in us that He went to the cross for us. Because of His sacrifice, we were changed by the "Big C" church and the local church and we want to join in this work. Even though we can never repay the sacrifice that He made for us, we can still give back to His church.

We have all heard the statistics that churches are dying all around the world. We refuse to believe that because the Bride will never die. However it is a sad epidemic that we are witnessing today and we want to do whatever we can to impact the Kingdom for Christ. Even if it means changing the status quo. We cannot settle and get comfortable because the enemy is still lurking. So many are walking away from the church and so many churches are closing their doors permanently. The question is what can we do to change this alarming trend? We are fully aware that God doesn't need us to help in the battle, but He desires for us to be about His business. We are willing to take the leap to the deep to partner with Him, are you willing to go with us?

I'm Afraid for Your Church

We recently partnered with 2 districts within the Church of The Nazarene to provide coaching and support to over 100 churches. We've already done evaluations at several and many more on the schedule. Every 4 years their denomination gathers to discuss the state of their denomination and where they are headed as a group. Since we are forming this partnership, we wanted to listen in on a few of their sessions during their General Assembly. We heard a staggering statistic from David Busic, one of six General Superintendents, that in 2016 24% of Nazarene Churches (5,353) reported having 0 people between the ages of 12-29 in their congregation.

In 2016 24% of Nazarene Churches (5,353) reported having 0 people between the ages of 12-29 in their congregation. - David Busic

Let the seriousness of that stat sink in. 0 people between 12-29 in 24% of an entire denomination of churches. That's code red. If we evaluated the statistics of many denominations and churches, we would find the same disturbing trend. Millennials are not going to church as much as the previous generation. These churches are becoming museums dedicated to the past. They are not world-changing movements. Something has to change.

As scary as those stats sound, it's not too late. There's still time to make course corrections and begin to reach a new generation of worshippers. Every time we visit a church that is in decline, we hear the same thing: "What do we do? How can we reverse the trend?" There's no magic formula, but there are a few key things that must happen to reverse the trend. Here are 3 critical steps to reaching a new generation for Christ.

1. Sense of Urgency

So many of our churches, pastors, and leaders are gingerly walking through life without a real sense of urgency about the mission they are called to. If we really believe Romans 6:23 is true, we're gonna need to get off our Blessed Assurance and do everything we can, short of sin, to reach as many people as possible for Christ. Every decision we make as a church needs to have a sense of urgency connected to reaching people that are not within the walls of our churches. We can never be satisfied with our current reality. We must keep pressing toward the prize! Set goals, work as a team, and go after it. When you reach it, move the line and do it again. If people can't get behind reaching people for Jesus, it might be time for them to find a new place to worship.

2. Strong Leadership

Show me a church that lacks urgency and you will probably find leaders who lack urgency. Everything rises and falls on leadership. People are attracted to strong, passionate leaders. Lead Pastors need to be downloading the vision from God for their church, inspiring their leadership to jump on board with the vision, and mobilizing their church to accomplish the mission that God has presented to their congregation.
Leadership is not for the weak or faint-hearted. We've got to lead strong. As I heard Eric Geiger recently say "If you want everyone to like you, go sell ice cream!" We hear so often about the struggles between pastors and leadership teams. It's time to put egos and agendas aside and get back to the Great Commission and Great Commandment. No more country club mentality. We're building hospitals for hurting people. We need men and women to lead strong to let the world know there's a place where they belong, especially the next generation. I want to see pastors and leaders who are willing to step up and let go of some things they love (tradition, creature comforts, and personal preference) for things they should love even more (young people connecting to Christ, missional movement, and baptisms).

3. Who's Up Next?

If I went to your church this weekend, how many people under the age of 30 would be leading in a significant way? I'm not talking about passing out the bulletin or sweeping up the lobby. I'm talking about leading the worship, directing the kids ministry, mentoring students, and even preaching the message. Having responsibility is a key to helping the next generation stick. They thrive on a sense of purpose. If your worship leader hasn't developed a young person to walk with them, it's time. If your student pastor hasn't mentored a young man or woman to lead other students, it's time. If you haven't given someone younger than you a chance to share the message, it's time. Sure, it might not be as good as you or your older leaders can do it (it might be better!?!), but you were young once and had to make some mistakes along the way. We've got to give leadership away and teach a new generation to love serving Jesus just as much as we do!

The thing that lit me(Chris) on fire to serve Christ as a 17 year old was the investment of the pastor who led me to Jesus. He took time to pray with me, teach me to serve and read the Bible, gave me opportunities for real leadership, and loved me through the rough times. I'm not afraid for the "Capital C" Church. It will be fine. It's been fine for 2,000 years. If you find your church is one that falls into the previously mentioned category, I'm afraid for your church. You're on a fast track to fading into the sunset and becoming a museum that pays tribute to the good old days. I don't know about you, but I'm not here to build museums, I'm here to build the church and equip the leaders. That's why we started The Ministry Mechanics. We are here to help churches reach their full potential. To help them thrive and not merely survive. We really believe that the local church is the hope of the world.

Building the Framework

When you are building anything whether it be a house, a car and yes even a church, the frame has to go up first. This doesn't just relate to the physical structure but also the organizational structure. Think about it, you can't invite someone to a house that doesn't have a frame because when the storms come you will get wet. You also can't let someone ride in a car with no framework. If you do, you won't get very far. The same is true with a church, we want to invite people to our church before we have the infrastructure built. When this happens, we aren't ready for guests and they usually come one time and never return. On the other end of the spectrum, many churches make the all too common mistake of growing too fast too soon without building the proper systems and the infrastructure that will sustain growth. This is why it is crucial for churches to build the infrastructure before they build the crowd.

Now we know there will be some that will debate this philosophy and we will receive pushback. They will say as long as we have a bible and Jesus that is all that we need. They might even quote the scripture, "Where two or more are gathered in His name, He will be there." Yes we believe that scripture too and we know that God can move anywhere and at anytime. We also know that God blesses preparation and hard work. He is not the author of chaos and He blesses us when we plan. Proverbs 16:3 says *Put God in charge of your work, then what you've planned will take place.*" This certainly doesn't mean whatever you wish He will command as if He is a spiritual genie. He just simply wants to bless your plans if your plans are in line with His purpose. God himself was very meticulous and strategic when it came to creation. It was done with order and in order. All throughout scripture, you will find God giving and blessing strategic plans. A great example of this was Noah who was given the schematics for the ark down to the cubit. Through His obedience and God's plans, the world was changed.

In the church today we don't see the necessity of building quality systems. In some ways we feel that if it's not broke we don't need to fix it without realizing that many times it's broken. If you aren't reaching people and seeing life change take place year after year, then what you are doing isn't working. To reach different people you will have to try different things. If you keep doing what you're doing, then you will keep getting what you are getting. Building systems that matter is crucial to any church's growth process, systems that are not complicated and are easily transferrable to many. Typical systems for churches today would include security, retention, outreach, leadership development/discipleship and first impressions, among others. One of the things The Ministry Mechanics is most passionate about is helping churches define and implement quality systems for growth. We realize how important it is to the longevity of the church. Please understand this isn't just for church plants but also for existing churches. It's never too late to put in the right systems and infrastructure.

Next Steps

Committed Christians are hard to come by these days. The average church goer is getting less and less committed and attends a service 1.5 times a month. Only around 20-25% of Americans are attending church 3 out of every 8 Sundays and that number continues to fall. We can accept these declining realities or we can do something about it. The challenge is getting people from being a spectator to actually getting in the game. We need to make people understand that it's a whole lot more fulfilling and more fun to play in the game than to watch. This happens by connecting people to the lifeblood of the church. Something special happens when you see the light come on in someone's heart and they become truly connected to the body. If you connect people to their passions and gifts then they will become committed to the church.

Getting people connected to their next step is essential when you are trying to get people to stick with your church. We must realize that each step isn't linear, it's very fluid and each person will be on a different path and step in the process. For some people salvation may be their next step, for others it could be to join a small group. You must create an environment where it's ok to belong before you believe. For someone, baptism could be the next step or maybe they have never given to the church and they want to become a contributor for the first time. You must make it easy for everyone in your church to take their next step whatever and whenever that may be. Your role as a church is to create opportunities for people to take that step. When this happens you will begin to see people more often, because they will be engaged as a part of something bigger than themselves rather than a bystander on the sideline.

The Curse of Complacency

Not only is building systems crucial to the overall design of the church, so is vision casting toward the future. Over the last 20 years, there are organizations that have been so occupied by their present and less concerned about their future. They got comfortable with their current situation and for some organizations they were lulled to sleep. Once very successful companies didn't continue to evolve and discover their space in their markets and some paid the ultimate price for those decisions. Thriving businesses that simply lost their identity and then lost their influence and finally in turn lost everything.

A great example of this was a little company called Blockbuster Video. They thought they had it all figured it out and they began to get fat and happy with the current climate. In the 80's and 90's Blockbuster Video was a major part of a typical Friday night. In most families, you to rented a movie and then picked up pizza and that was a big night. It certainly wasn't an overnight decline, but it sure seemed like it. The world changed and Blockbuster stayed the same. Same business model, same look, same employees, nothing changed. Everything else was changing quickly, other companies were coming in and not just competing with Blockbuster but these other video companies were changing the entire game. It wasn't like Home Depot and Lowe's where they had similar models. Someone figured out a whole new delivery method for renting movies from the comfort of your own home. Some genius thought if pizza could be delivered why couldn't the movie? It wasn't too much longer that the powerful Blockbuster was a distant memory and found their way out of business. They vanished nearly without any warning, pretty soon Netflix, Hulu and Amazon became part of our normal lexicon in America. All because Blockbuster was complacent with where they were and they weren't concerned about where they were going and how to adapt to their unique communities and the culture.

So what does this have to do with the church? It's simple: complacency is the death of many churches. Churches that were so content with the success of their past that they mailed it in and became stagnant. Churches that failed to realize that the world is changing around us but refused to adapt their methods to reach those who are far from Christ. Expecting people to run to us, rather than taking grace and love to them. I'm not talking about changing the Gospel or even watering it down, I'm not talking theology at all. I'm talking about realizing that things can change quickly and if we as the church remain complacent, time will pass us by. If you don't believe me, notice all of the church buildings closing in America. Most denominations reported losses in worship attendance and baptisms last year in the United States. We can deny it and ignore it, but we will become Blockbuster Video, irrelevant and a distant memory of the past if we don't wake up the Church today. We need to have a sense of urgency to break out of our complacent state and truly live out the mission. We must continue to innovate and discover new ways to reach people in this ever-changing world.

When I was a younger associate pastor I worked for a church that was the model for a church that became complacent. They were a typical downtown church who thought it would be a great idea to move out to the suburbs. They bought the land, built the building and made the move. The church exploded over the next few years but it wasn't long before the church became fine with what they had. They never thought to build the infrastructure for the growth and they couldn't handle the influx of people. After a few missteps by the leadership, the church began to decline, less than 5 years after they moved into the building. The building was the vision, once they built it the vision was over in their minds. They didn't understand that the vision was just beginning. They failed to realize that the building can't be the vision, it was a resource to fulfill the vision. They were comfortable in the fancy new building but they assumed that alone would get people to come through their doors. It did at first, but the Field of Dreams method is never a great long term solution. If you build the building, they will come, but will they stay? Many times the answer is no without a fresh vision that continues. Unfortunately this church went from over 1000 in attendance to around 400 in less than two years. Thankfully now they have recovered but it took almost a decade and they are still not to the level that they once were.

Complacency is dangerous in churches today. As a church you must be aware of this weapon even when you are at the height of your success. That's the moment, that you pour on more vision, not sit on the vision that got you to that place. Move forward, don't stand still and watch the rest of the world pass you by. Keep casting the vision even when feel you are on top of the world. What is the vision that you have for your church and your city? If we have a bigger vision for your church than you have for your church, then Houston we have a problem.

Create the Space

I was listening to a podcast recently called *How I Built This*, it's an interview show with some of the brightest entrepreneurs and they share how they built their company. On this particular episode the founder of a major company was talking about one of her greatest challenges which was creating a space in the market for her product. It made me think, this is one of the biggest challenges in churches today, discovering our space in our community. Even though Jesus and the church isn't a product, as the church we still must find what makes our local church tick and what sets us apart. There are many churches who just don't know who they are and don't have a clue where they are going, churches with very little strategy to reach lost people for Christ. When leaders can't discover a vision of their own, they borrow one from their neighbor. So many churches today are trying to look at what the big church in town is doing and then they try to mimic the big brother. That rarely works out too well.

In the world today, we have all types of people, which means we need all types of churches that are uniquely wired to reach their unique community. Ask yourself the question: What makes our church unique? When you discover the answer to this question you will then create the space in your community for your church. It doesn't really matter what it is, just as long as you define who you are and where you are going. Once you discover your space in your community, you will begin to understand who your target audience is and how to reach them more effectively. The wider the net you cast and the more you try to be all things to all people, the more frustrating it will become for your church and for you as a leader. In fact when you throw out the wider net on a vague target audience and your vision becomes less than laser focused, stagnation begins to set into your church. Trust me, you don't want that.

Reach More Lost People

Once you have discovered your identity, determined who you are trying to reach, built systems that matter, and casted vision, now it's time to get going. The gospel is the greatest news that we could ever tell and we should proclaim it confidently with a sense of urgency. We must embody and live the Great Commission as a church, which is:

"Therefore go and make disciples of all nations, baptizing them in the name of the Father and of the Son and of the Holy Spirit, and teaching them to obey everything I have commanded you. And surely I am with you always, to the very end of the age." - Matthew 28:19-20

The question is how can we reach the nations, if we can't reach our neighbors? That's where it starts. Whoever your defined target audience is, that's where we must go first. It starts with us praying for the people that God will put in our path as individuals and as a church. We make the mistake of inviting people to church without investing in their life. If we were to pray, invest and then invite and allow God to move in that process, then we would see life change take place. I'm all for inviting people to church, but if it's just a random invite, it wont be as effective as it would be from a person that has prayed and invested in their life.

A while back we began to think about the heartbeat and common thread of most of our partner churches. It was simply this, "To reach more lost people for Jesus." Whenever someone asks why we do what we do or why we are making a change, the answer is always the same: "To reach more lost people." That is why we the believers of Jesus Christ are put here on this earth. That is the purpose that should flow through every major decision and anything we do within the church. If we want to join God in the mission of Building the Church, we must be about reaching more lost people and expanding the Kingdom. We still believe in the local church and believe that her greatest days are not in the past but rather ahead. We want to see more people join in this mission that we are so passionate about.

EQUIP THE LEADER

CHAPTER 13

THE MINISTRY MECHANICS

As a result, it has become clear throughout the whole palace guard and to everyone else that I am in chains for Christ. Because of my chains, most of the brothers in the Lord have been encouraged to speak the word of God more courageously and fearlessly. **Philippians 1:13-14**

Have you ever wondered, what sets apart the mega-church from the small church? There has to be a quality that is a common thread throughout most, if not all successful churches. What is it? Is it money? Probably not, because at one time the mega-church had to be a small church and didn't have a lot of money. Is it location? No, location helps to some degree but that is never a determining growth factor. Is it a building? No, because some churches begin in a garage or a storefront. I have come to the realization that what sets these churches apart is simply Spirit-led fearless leadership. Leadership that is never wavering or indecisive. Leadership that never dwells only on the present but is always thinking about the future. Leadership that knows every wrinkle of God's revelation to them and expounds it clearly to their people. A leader who relies on that very revelation to move inside and through them, instead of constantly being inspired by the latest book or method. A leader that doesn't cower at the thought of difficult decisions. A leader of a successful church takes every opportunity to follow the Holy Spirit's leading.

If you take a look at Craig Groeschel, Ed Young, Steven Furtick, Andy Stanley or any great church leader today, you will find the quality of being fearless. Each of these men lead some of the largest churches in America, but they didn't start large, they were built from the ground up. It began as an audacious dream and they were and still are not afraid to speak the truth or step on toes. When the truth is on your side, it is easy to be fearless. As leaders we sometimes let people, boards, big givers, denominational restrictions and other outside entities get to us and sometimes takes us off mission. We forget that being fearless is a part of our DNA. Those who are called have this deep passion within to be courageous and fearless, although sometimes we forget that we have it.

If pleasing God and not worrying so much about pleasing people is our priority, then we will be obedient to that burning desire within us to be fearless. Craig Groeschel says, "Becoming obsessed with what people think is the quickest way to forget about what God thinks."

So are you fearless? If the answer is, "well, I used to be," then you need to find out what happened and try to regain that passion. Discover where you got off track, who you started trying to impress, who your audience became as you got distracted from your calling from God. If the answer to the fearless question is yes, then become the leader that God has called you to be. Lead someone to Christ, lead your team, start a church or just be faithful in the one you are already leading. Do whatever it takes to be a fearless leader.

We are taught in 2 Timothy 1:7, *"For God has not given us a spirit of fear and timidity, but of power, love, and self-discipline."* God has given us a bold faith and He wants us to be bold leaders. Each step on your path to becoming a great leader is a bold leap of faith. At times, you will be going down a path that might seem unconventional. If you want to be a great leader, you sometimes must travel in unmarked territories and create a new path that has not yet been made. When you are bold in the face of the unknown, it will inspire your team to have courage and will encourage them to keep going when things get difficult. We all know that difficulty is inevitable; it is a defining trademark of this life on earth.

Max Lucado says, "A man who wants to lead the orchestra must turn his back on the crowd." This requires complete trust in God and a bold leader who believes in the vision that God has given. This doesn't mean to completely turn your back on people, but when the desires of people outrank the desires of God, then you must make a decision that might seem unpopular to some. If the decision is handled the right way, with love and humility, then God will bless you as you follow His lead.

The Catch 22 for most pastors is that they know changes and difficult decisions need to be made, but they are strapped with fear of other people's opinions or people who contribute to their church. Earlier this year we wrote a blog post related to the devastating church numbers that we mentioned in the previous chapter and the need to change the way we were doing things as the church today so we can reverse the trend. While many responded favorably to this post, there was one that didn't totally buy into it. It was a pastor's wife that said that she didn't want her church to make the changes that were required to reverse the statistics. Her reasoning was that the older folks in her congregation would leave and those were the people who were paying the bills. She said that, "She didn't want to die on that hill." The more and more that I thought about that statement, the more it bothered me. In ministry, that's the hill we are called to die on. To be obedient and to do whatever it takes to reach people for Christ even if it means making changes. Galatians 1:10-12 in the Message says, *"Do you think I speak this strongly in order to manipulate crowds? Or curry favor with God? Or get popular applause? If my goal was popularity, I wouldn't bother being Christ's slave. Know this—I am most emphatic here, friends—this great Message I delivered to you is not mere human optimism. I didn't receive it through the traditions, and I wasn't taught it in some school. I got it straight from God, received the Message directly from Jesus Christ."*

Paul was seeking to bring people to obedience not of man, but of God. When we get so focused on people pleasing, we ignore God's will for our life and our church. Paul was singularly focused on pleasing God, even if He had to turn His back on the crowd who were just concerned about themselves. Their preferences, their needs, their desires, we humans often look to these things rather than seeking God's desires. We must learn that the church isn't about us, even though we live in a "me" culture. It's about dropping our desires and taking up the desires of God together as one body. When someone gets upset at a new direction or a change, selfishness is exposed and the spotlight is turned on them rather than God who rightfully deserves the attention. Change is coming. When it does, what hill will you choose to die on as a leader?

Embrace Change

"If we are to better the future, we must disturb the present." C. Booth

Leaders who embrace change are the leaders that will build longevity in ministry and be successful in the long run. We should never underestimate the power of change. Change is hard and it has been since the beginning of time. In 1829, Martin Van Buren, then the governor of New York, sent a letter of resistance to change to President Andrew Jackson.

"Mr. President, railroad carriages are pulled at the enormous speed of 15 miles per hour by engines which, in addition to endangering life and limb of passengers, roar and snort their way through the countryside, setting fires to crops, scaring the livestock and frightening women and children. The almighty certainly never intended the people should travel at such breakneck speeds." M. Van Buren, 1829, Governor of New York

The blazing speed of 15 miles per hour doesn't seem like much, but it was enough to cause Martin Van Buren to write a letter to the president about it. If poor Martin was around today, he wouldn't know what to think about a jumbo jet or a high speed rail.

Look at the change we have experienced with the Word of God, which was once written on scrolls. Now you can read the Bible in any translation on any device that you own. No one would've thought when the Guttenberg printing press was released that we would be reading the very same words on a handheld device. The church itself has gone through many changes over the years and we passed the test of those changes eventually with flying colors.

One thousand years into the church, everyone stood up the entire time. Then there was the invention of the pew. I'm sure there was one guy in the congregation at that time who said, "If they get pews, I'm outta there!" In 1361, this massive instrument called the pipe organ was introduced to what I would imagine was groans and jeers. It was probably the major dispute within the church that year. Fast forward to 1900, air conditioning was introduced in the more fancy churches. I'm sure it took longer for the country churches to catch on to that. Today we couldn't fathom going to church without AC and we certainly couldn't attend church without a chair.

Throughout time, change has been navigated by churches and churches are still here. Change and Jesus have been the only constants throughout the church's history. Change is a good thing and every leader must be the tip of the spear that is the catalyst for change. It is healthy for organisms to change and grow and most times we must change in order to grow. The human body is designed to grow and as we go through this process of life, things begin to change. We are not designed to stay the same. The same is true with the body of Christ, we must go through the process of change and that translates into growth. If the church doesn't find ways to relate to the current, ever-changing culture, then we will fall into the trap of stagnation

Excuses for Change

Each week as church consultants we hear so many reasons why leaders won't make changes within their church. Most of the time the answers are the same from leader to leader. We both fully understand the pressure and the weight that each leader is responsible for. We have both been Lead Pastors and have felt that enormous elephant on your back. However we also knew that God led us to those positions. We believed then and still firmly believe now in His power that nothing is too hard for Him. He never fails us even when we feel overwhelmed. When we have God on our side and He is leading the way, no excuse against change is valid.

Most of the justification for stagnation that we hear involves other people. The two biggest ones are "My Leadership team won't buy into drastic changes" and "The older folks will get mad or won't like it." In both cases it's sometimes how we communicate the change that is more important than the change itself. You would benefit greatly by bringing the opposition alongside this exciting mission rather than competing with their opinions. Listen to their side and then unite. When you communicate it with clarity and passion and when you reinforce the idea that we are doing this to reach more lost people, then they might begin to see the vision that God has given you. If they don't, then remember that you are not always going to please everyone.

The early 20th century journalist, Herbert Swope said, "I cannot give you the formula for success, but I can give you the formula for failure, which is: Try to please everybody." This is always a dangerous game to play, because it is impossible to please everyone. Many times what happens is churches cater to the one angry person who wants his way, rather than the masses who are hungry to chase after the will of God. When this happens, the mission and vision are derailed. These churches go down a dangerous path of destruction and become out of step with the direction that God is taking them. Their inaction because of the minority alone is still an action, in the wrong direction. Every time you choose not to change something, you are also choosing to keep it the same.

My friend Pastor Rick Howerton once said, "Churches that are unwilling to change ultimately do change…they transition from effective to ineffective to dead."
Don't be that church!
Start Here

There are other leaders that recognize the need to change, they have the desire to do something about it, they just don't know where to start. Anytime I attend a new church, there is always a bit of apprehension and anxiety, simply because I don't know anyone and I don't have a clue where anything is. Let's face it, most churches have someone to open the door for you, but after that, it's a no holds barred survival of the fittest. If there aren't any signs that tell where I need to go, that just raises my blood pressure to epic proportions. Then I went to one unnamed church that had a sign in the parking lot, yes the parking lot that simply said, "Start here!" You couldn't miss this sign, it was bold and just screamed

141

out, "I'm here and I will take your anxiety now." It was the best first impressions experience in the history of the American church. Ok I could be exaggerating, but it was fantastic. I felt like I belonged from the first moment.

I think many of us want to make changes in our church but we don't know where to start. You might be overwhelmed and feel buried under the weight of busyness, clutter, responsibilities and a calendar that just won't seem to clear. We meet pastors every day in this category. You could be like I was, just searching for the "start here" sign.

Maybe strategy or honest evaluation isn't your problem, maybe it's just simply execution. Your favorite football team may have the greatest coach in the world with the most extensive play book. He may be an offensive genius with plays that will most certainly work; however if there isn't proper execution, it's a moot point. The greatest strategy and plays will be wasted because you failed to do your part and execute. I can handle someone giving it their all and coming up short, but what I can't handle is someone that has everything they need to be successful and they don't do anything about it.

Simply start with one small thing. At times we have a list of things that we need to change within our church and we don't know what to do first. Just pick one and go with it. When that one is completed, go down your list and knock the next one out. After awhile you will have your list completed and then you will be ready to put some new things on the list. You should never use the excuse of where do I start. Just start and watch God help you throughout the process of making the right changes. Remember if He calls you to it, He will always give you everything you need to complete the task and He will never leave you alone while you are following His will. Trust Him and lead with boldness.

Pass the Baton to the Next Generation

Something happens when a leader gets to a certain age. Some leaders who are self aware willingly develop leaders to replace them one day. They give a clear path for the transition of authority over to the ones that they have invested in. Then on the other end of the spectrum, we have a generation of leaders who are white knuckling the keys to all the way to the grave. They have no interest in developing leaders. Which leads me to ask the question, if you aren't developing leaders can you really call yourself a leader? A leader's job isn't just to lead others, but to develop others to lead.

Wise Leaders Have a Clear Succession Plan.

Walt Disney was one of the greatest leaders of the last century, if not the greatest. I don't think there is a person living in the free world who doesn't know who Walt Disney is and what he created. Most of us know the legacy that he left and many of us have visited one of the theme parks that bears his name.

However the man who created the famous mouse was once fired at a Kansas City newspaper for lacking ideas and not being creative enough. Can you imagine telling Walt Disney himself that he's not creative and that he didn't have any ideas worthy of the local newspaper? The rest is history. He used that rejection as fuel for his motivation to succeed. What most of the world doesn't know is how his life ended and what happened to his business following his sudden death in 1966.

Walt Disney died unexpectedly at a relatively young age, only ten days after his 65th birthday. A month prior to his death, he was diagnosed with lung cancer which attributed to his demise. At the time of Walt's death, the Disney company was doing very well and it had achieved incredible success for nearly 30 years. However when Walt died, the company almost died as well. For 19 years the company went on a steady decline and nearly went bankrupt. Yes the major conglomerate that we know today almost went down the drain.

I'm sure there were many factors that contributed to this state of ineptitude at the Disney company. Lack of inspiration, maybe

Walt's vision wasn't transferred properly or they might've had a culture problem, which is very common. The fact was Walt died and the company was caught without a plan. A true succession plan to carry the organization to the next generation. A plan that would move the company forward despite the leader. Some say Walt Disney thought of himself as invincible, which we all know is the greatest fantasy of all.

In our churches and organizations today, we are seeing the same type of issue. Many leaders feel there is no need for a plan of succession. They have the mindset that they will always be around and to think beyond their own mortality or relevancy isn't needed. This line of thinking couldn't be further from the truth. Fortunately for the Disney company, they were able to survive the 19 years of gradual decline. Most churches couldn't survive two years of decline let alone two decades.

When ego and arrogance get in the way of wisdom and sound judgment, decline happens. I've seen too many pastors who have mistakenly held onto the baton to the next generation until it was too late. It affected their legacy, but more importantly it tarnished the local church. Hand over the baton to the next generation before you take it to the grave with you. Identify a Godly leader, someone you can believe in, invest in and change your story. You get the chance to create the narrative of how your last chapter of ministry will be told. Put a plan in place long before you are ready to leave and God will give you the right time to pass the baton to the next generation of leaders.

Wise leaders know the proper time to pass the baton and know how important it is to have a legacy plan in place. Similar to a relay race, if you wait too long to pass the baton to the next person, you will be called for a foul and be disqualified from the race. Make sure the passing of the baton is smooth and you give them a running start to propel them to greater things in the next chapter. You don't want to drop the baton or hold onto it for too long; it might get ugly if you do. Instead of being a detriment to your successor, be a blessing and propel that person to more success than you could ever imagine for yourself.

Not only should you bless your successor with a smooth transition, you should continue to bless that person long after you are gone. The greatest thing your successor could say about you is that you were their greatest cheerleader from the sidelines. That doesn't mean you have to stick around, that means your role dramatically changes and that you provide support in any way possible. Prepare them from the beginning of the transition plan and then release them. After you release them, cheer them on with everything that's inside of you and be proud that you chose to go this route rather than be caught unprepared or even worse, unwilling to pass the baton. Don't let the way you step out damage your legacy by not finishing well.

Building a Deep Farm System

We love the game of baseball. It is always a fun day when we go to a day game and have lunch in center field at Minute Maid Park in Houston as we watch the Astros play. There is nothing quite like it, so relaxing and laid back, especially when the retractable roof is closed. While the weather in Houston soars over 100 degrees in the summer at times, it's nice to watch baseball inside at 70 degrees.

Looking back through the years at all of the great baseball teams, the really great ones were teams that were developed over time. The teams that spent the most energy developing talent were the ones that ended up winning. If your team was successful it was because they had a great farm system of younger players that trained hard and then were ready to play in the Major Leagues. Baseball called their minor leagues the farm system because of a joke in the 1930's. At that time, St. Louis Cardinals general manager Branch Rickey organized teams in small towns and would quip that they, "were growing players down on the farm like corn." Once the players grow and are ready to play, they would bring them up to the Major League club. If you think about it anything on a farm is something that is grown, developed and cultivated.

In baseball, the deeper you can build your farm system, the more successful the organization will be. Those are usually the teams that win championships. What if we built our leadership development system like a farm system? Always developing, cultivating and growing leaders. If this were to happen in churches, you would never have a shortage a great leaders. The deeper the farm system in your church, the more successful you will become in discipling others and equipping leaders for service. The moment that you as a leader understand the value of building a deep farm system is the very moment that will transform your church and community. God did not pour leadership skills into you to keep them to yourself. John Maxwell says, "A leader who produces other leaders multiplies their influences." Find ways to multiply yourself and repeat it over and over again.

Here are three keys to building a deep farm system in your church:

1. Identifying Talent

It starts with identifying potential leaders that are around you. At times as leaders we tend to see more in someone than they see in themselves. We must be aware of potential in others and call it out when we see it. Someone in your church may not have the confidence yet to lead; maybe your encouragement will prompt them to lead. They may have a gift that hasn't been cultivated and needs to be unearthed by you. There is so much untapped potential out there, we are just unaware and not intentionally looking for it. It's not just up to you, but you must build up your farm system to implement and begin the leadership multiplication process.

There are also those out there who feel unworthy or unfit to lead. We must look for the prospects that others don't value. In baseball, this is something that good owners and general managers excel at doing. They will find players who other teams don't want and turn them into stars. I have seen it many times. In the church, we must discover people who feel that God can't use them. Those people that feel like they are in the margins. I (Jeremy) felt this way. The enemy told me the same lies and I had someone like Chris tell me that God was going to use me in greater ways. I've seen God change people and use them to build the Kingdom throughout my life. Jentzen Franklin says, "The best bad people, make the best good people." This is so true. If you are reading this book and that hits a chord with you, then God has greater plans in store for you. Your leadership journey isn't over. You can still lead with greater influence that ever before.

2. Developing Talent

Once you identify potential leaders, it's time to develop them. The farm system is the best place for them to grow. Much like the minor leagues in baseball, it will give leaders a chance to lead on a smaller scale. It could be a small group leader or volunteering in the kid's ministry. A smaller role doesn't mean it's any less significant. It's just a place to start until they are ready for more responsibility. As they grow in their walk with Christ and as they strengthen their leadership capabilities, they may discover a burning desire in their heart to lead in a different area than they originally planned. The key to developing leaders during this stage of the game is to make sure they are appreciated and encouraged. It costs absolutely zero dollars to encourage someone and tell them they are doing an awesome job. Everyone wants to feel appreciated. Don't miss this opportunity to show love to the ones that you are developing.

3. Let Them Play

Once the leaders are identified and developed, it's time to put them in the game and let them play. Now it's their job to begin the development process again, this time by cultivating someone else. The role is reversed. That doesn't mean that you stop growing and developing, as we all know that never stops. It just simply means that you will begin to replicate yourself repeatedly. This type of development strategy is contagious and you will want to continue to develop others. That's what leaders do and that is the essential component that will make you a true leader.

One thing is for sure, God did not call you to be a mediocre leader that leads a mediocre church or organization. It's time that you take your leadership to the next level. It's time that you become the fearless leader that God calls you to be and because of that calling you can begin to build other fearless leaders who are passionate about building even more fearless leaders. Pretty soon the spark will become a wildfire that cannot be contained. Your church will be transformed, your community will take notice and more importantly Heaven will be aware of your passion to build leaders.

WHAT WE DO

CHAPTER 14

THE MINISTRY MECHANICS

As we wind down this book, we wanted to leave you with ways that we can partner with you as a leader and with your church. We fully realize that ministry is hard, but the great news is, you don't have to do it alone. As we have written repeatedly in this book, we are passionate about building the church and equipping the leader. We have the desire to be a part of your story as you change your church, your community and the world. There are four primary tools we use to build churches and equip leaders. Weekend Service Evaluation, Virtual Executive Pastor, Staffing Solutions and Leadership Tune-Ups. One thing is for sure, we are always better together.

Weekend Service Evaluation

Have you ever wondered what it's like for a first-time guest to attend your church? Now you can know exactly what they experience! We utilize a tool called Weekend Service Evaluation to evaluate various processes and ministries in your church. One of our team members will visit your church and look at everything through a lens that helps you reach your goals. Much like a secret shopper would come into a retail store to evaluate the experience, our team comes into your church incognito to do the same. Ready to go multi-site? Ready to grow? Ready to make a significant programming change? Start with a Weekend Service Evaluation to get things moving in the right direction. We'll help you:

1. Determine Your Next Strategic Step

It always starts with vision. Learning what's next for your church can be a daunting discovery process. We can come alongside you and help you assess your strengths and weaknesses. We'll also help you decipher the God-given vision for your church or organization.

2. Evaluate the Church

Everything from kids check-in to the message will get a look from the viewpoint of a new person in your church. You"ll receive a full and comprehensive report on every area we assess. It may sound terrifying, but in the end, you'll find it to be one of the most encouraging experiences. We'll help you evaluate your current programs and compare them to the next strategic steps you want to take as a church.

3. Create an Action Plan

What's next? We'll help you create an action plan to lean into those strengths and improve on areas of weakness. Having a clear picture of current reality is one of the most important tools for any organization that wants to take the next steps in accomplishing their goals and dreams. Once we're done, you'll have tangible and concrete steps that will help you move your church forward.

We recently did a Weekend Service Evaluation for a church that had plateaued for a while. One of the first things we noticed when we walked in the foyer of the church was a clear eyesore. It was a bookshelf with out-of-date magazines and random old books. It was apparent that no one had touched this area in quite a while. When we finished the report, we mentioned it to the pastor and he hadn't noticed this area because in his eyes the eyesore had blended into the environment. Most churches have their version of the bookshelf. It may be something that the leadership hasn't noticed but others might have, especially first time guests. Sometimes organizations don't realize things need to be changed because after a while it begins to blend into the culture.

Earlier this year we were in The Galleria mall food court in Houston and we noticed a particular sign that caught our eye. It was the month of March and a particular chain restaurant had a sign advertising, "Catering for your Christmas party." Here we were three months removed from Christmas and still no one within the organization noticed. It took a fresh set of eyes from the outside of the organization to spot it immediately. As we walked by, we noticed the error in about three seconds. This is why you need a fresh set of eyes looking at your weekend experience. We don't want to just critique, we want to find ways to enhance the experience. It also could be something that you have noticed but don't know how to change, so you leave it alone and hope no one else notices. What we fail to realize is that everything matters when you are trying to make the Sunday experience excellent. Our goal is never to simply point the negative out, we will also affirm the things that we love about the experience. We will also never just give you a list of things to change without giving you a solution to the problem.

Here are three things that a fresh set of eyes brings to your church:

Credibility

When you bring in a fresh set of eyes, you should bring in someone who has seen many environments and someone who knows what to look for at your church. The Ministry Mechanics provide that type of experience. We will look at your situation through the eyes of a first time guest. We will also look at it through the lens of the church's vision. This is important when assessing a Sunday experience. By bringing someone in from the outside, you bring an unbiased, open minded and experienced point of view into your church that will give you a very honest and accurate evaluation of where you are as a church.

Clarity

A fresh set of eyes also provides clarity. You will discover some of the things that you need to add or subtract to enhance your church. It will provide a clear understanding for your team to make the necessary changes. An outside perspective will give you a clear picture of your current reality and help clarify the necessary steps for growth.

Creativity

Fresh eyes can provide concrete and creative solutions to problems within the church. An outside source of creativity can be healthy for churches, especially smaller churches who unfortunately don't have the staff that can provide a mass pool of ideas. The Ministry Mechanics can become this source for creative solutions for your church.

The misnomer of bringing in a consultant from the outside, is the assumption that there must be something wrong if you are bringing in a fresh set of eyes. Actually this couldn't be further from the truth. If you feel that your church is in a place of strength, our desire is to make it only stronger. The Weekend Service Evaluation is the first step in the right direction. If you want to go deeper than just the weekend, an in-depth, full church assessment may be helpful in determining the health and direction of your church.

Virtual Executive Pastor ™

Virtual Executive Pastor is the best way for a leader to focus all their energy on their strengths and off load the things that they either don't enjoy doing or can't do. Wouldn't it be great to have an executive team without all of the overhead expense? The salaries of Executive Pastors in the US range from a low of $16,227 to a high of $433,458, with a median salary of $78,399. Let's face it, most churches cannot afford to pay anywhere near that salary for an executive pastor. That's just reality. We will provide this service with decades of executive experience for a fraction of the cost and the best part is we can do that virtually from anywhere in the world. If you need for us to be more hands on, we can handle that as well.

Are you needing to clarify your vision, values and mission? Are you wanting to build systems that will allow your church to reach its full potential? You do the dreaming and we help make it a reality. We would love to help your church establish a process and plan that will help you get to the next level. We can work with your leadership team, staff or entire church to teach on a variety of ideas.

Here are just a few of the areas of ministry that our team can assist with:

- HR Support
- Branding and Design
- Vision/Mission/Values
- Organizational Structure
- Building Systems
- Capital Campaigns
- Websites and Social Media
- Worship/Children/Finance Direction
- Programming
- Leadership Development

VXP Process

1. Clarify Your Purpose

One of the best things an organization can do is clarify the win. From the first day, one of our Virtual Executive Pastors or VXP's will help you craft concise statements that powerfully illustrate what success looks like for you, your team and your church. Clarifying the what, how and why will steer your organization in a positive direction for many years to come.

2. Pick the Process

After we clarify the win together, we will design custom systems such as next steps, first impressions, HR or a training track for your church. We have tons of resources at our fingertips. We'll find the right tools for you to build in accountability and direction in your programming and processes. This won't be a carbon copy process that we have used at a mega-church or another church, this will be customized specifically for your church's unique vision.

3. Define the Organization

Every organization must find the things that make them stand out and distinct in their communities. What does your church do that no one else does? Are you more evangelical or theological? Do you reach families or young people? What programs do you need to add or eliminate to reach your goals? We can help create the culture you've always dreamed of.

Staffing Solutions

When did finding a great team member get so complicated and expensive? The Ministry Mechanics are here to simplify the process with Staffing Solutions. Need help finding the next amazing member of your team? We can help! Our team will help you plan out your next hire and identify the right candidate for your opening.

We hear from church leaders quite often that the process that they have experienced previously has been expensive and very painstakingly difficult. We try to eliminate those two roadblocks from the process. You don't have to spend $30k on a staff search to find the right person. We like to keep things simple. Here's what you can expect with a Staffing Search led by us:

- Customized Job Description
- Candidates...Lots of candidates (300+ for Lead Pastors/200+ for Associate Pastors)
- 60+ years of ministry experience to help guide you through the process
- Reasonable fixed cost with no hidden fees
- 90 day guarantee - if it doesn't work out for any reason with the new hire, we'll start over until we get it right

Staffing Solution Process

1. Create the Profile

It all starts with developing a complete profile of the kind of leader you want for your organization. We'll help you craft a job description and put on paper the kinds of characteristics you're looking for in your candidate. We'll also spend lots of time with your leadership team, in person or on video conferencing, to get to know you and your church. The total timeline for an Associate Pastor hire is typically around 2-4 months. The total timeline for a Lead Pastor hire is typically around 3-6 months (every situation is unique, so times may vary by experience).

2. Gather Resumes

Once we have the profile, it's time to gather resumes. We'll get 50+ for Associate Pastor positions and 100+ for Lead Pastor positions from a host of sources. We'll forward all the resumes to your team. But, we'll recommend 5-10 of the best candidates to your team for evaluation, based on the profile. We'll evaluate every candidate and their qualifications through the filters developed from part one. This process usually takes around 1-3 months, depending on the position (every situation is unique, so times may vary by experience).

3. Interview Candidates

We'll setup video interviews with the best 4 or 5 with your leadership team. We'll open the conversation with some specific questions and then open it up to your team. Once you've narrowed your choices down to two, it's time for in-person interviews and background research. You'll fly the candidates in to spend time with them and check with their references. We'll provide a comprehensive background check for the final two candidates to assist in the decision. If you get to the final two and they aren't a good fit, we'll go back and keep looking until we find the right fit.

4. Make the Hire

Once you've prayed over and decided on a candidate, it's time to make the hire. We'll assist in getting the average salaries for similar positions in your city and the particular ministry position you're hiring. If you find out in the first 90 days that the new hire isn't a good fit, we'll get back to the drawing board and start again until we get it right.

Leadership Tune Ups

What is a "Tune-Up?" Tune-ups are leadership development sessions that cover 2-4 specific topics ranging from church growth and systems to church planting and building a launch team. Tune-Ups are a great way to begin a journey of growth and development for churches and their leaders. Every organization can benefit from an outside perspective from time to time. Our team has decades of combined ministry experience in a variety of different environments. Best of all, tune-up topics are fully customizable for the unique needs of you and your team and a lot of fun!

Topics can include: Breaking Through Stereotypes, Leading Strong, Invite Culture, Worship Stage Presence, Security & Safety, First-Impressions Training, Culture Killers, and anything you need help with.

Tune-ups are geared for existing churches ready to go to the next level or church plants that are gearing up for a successful launch. We are passionate to see both existing churches re-ignite as well as new churches planted in communities. The solution isn't one or the other, it's both.

Conclusion

We were having lunch one day shortly before we officially launched The Ministry Mechanics. We saw a local pastor named Andrew and began to make a connection. Just a few weeks later, Andrew's church became one of our first partner churches. We came in the picture three years after the launch of the church. When we came on board they seemed to hit a wall, which is not uncommon in today's church planting culture. They were at a crossroads and weren't seeing any movement taking place.

After doing a Weekend Service Evaluation we were able to pinpoint several areas that needed to be addressed. There were really no systems to speak of and no strategy for next steps. We knew this church could really use "Virtual Executive Pastor," so they agreed to continue our partnership. Over the course of a year our team devised a plan and became a part of their team, which was exactly what we wanted to do: Be a part of their team.

After the first year, Andrew, who had been losing hope when we started, began to feel so much more hopeful about where God was taking the church. He didn't need another conference or video training, he needed people that cared about him and stuck beside him even when times got tough.

We didn't want to give Andrew our vision for his church, because God had already given him a clear vision in his heart. We wanted to champion his vision and our desire was to simply help him take his vision from where they were to where they wanted to be. Our desire was to help him through the process and to put clear, realistic steps in place.

We live in the age of over-information. We have resources for days. There seems to be a conference that you could attend every week if you really wanted to. There are video modules for every topic. However we encounter pastors everyday that are simply overwhelmed with the amount of information even when the information is good. Don't get us wrong, we are not anti-resources, because you are reading one right now. The problem is when the resource that they learned from the mega-pastor at the conference doesn't work at their church, they begin to second guess everything. What they didn't know is that megachurch pastor is usually pastoring a church where the results are not typical.

We normally see pastors do one of two things. They try to do everything they learn, which doesn't really help them stay true to their vision and what God called them to do. That's simply trying to make a carbon copy of someone else's vision which rarely works. On the flip side, they do absolutely nothing because they don't know how to start or they don't feel they have the people or leadership to pull it off.

We've learned that most leaders don't have a problem finding resources or finding ways to grow their church. What most pastors and leaders need is someone to walk with them and encourage them throughout the process. We are just two guys that just want to genuinely help leaders and churches. We left jobs at a church with full benefits to take this leap of faith into the unknown because we no longer felt called to A single church, we felt the calling to serve THE CHURCH.

We have seen the research that the church is in decline. However, we refuse to believe the hyperbole that the church is dead. We believe in the local church and we believe that the greatest days of the local church are ahead. God chooses to use people like you to change the world and the bride of the Christ is the vehicle He uses to bring about that change. To see a single person cross over from death to life reaffirms to us why we do what we do. Hopefully this book has inspired you to keep pressing forward, to keep dreaming about ways to reach people for Christ and to continue to leap to the deep to reach the vision that God has put in your heart.

We believe in you and believe in your calling. We want to do more than just to inspire you to dream. We want to walk alongside you and partner together to......

Build the Church and Equip the Leader.

HOW IT WORKS

1. LET'S TALK

It starts with a conversation. We want to hear about your ministry and passion to find the best way we can partner to help your church or personal ministry reach a new level of influence.

2. PROPOSAL

After our conversation, we'll send you a proposal with every element we discuss and a detailed plan for success.

3. SIGN UP

If The Ministry Mechanics are right for you, we will send out a contract for you to sign. All you have to do is sign it digitally and we'll be ready to go.

4. CONNECT

Once a contract is signed, we'll schedule a time to research and get to work building a comprehensive plan for you or your organizaiton. We'll spend a lot of time and ask a lot of questions of you or people in your ministry. We want to get a full picture of the entire scope of the project.

5. GET TO WORK

Let's get started! We're ready to help you or your organization reach maximum potential. You'll have personal contact information of The Ministry Mechanics. You will be a part of our team and we will be a part of yours. We will work hard and celebrate all that God will do.

THEMINISTRYMECHANICS.COM

Jeremy's Acknowledgements

I want to thank my amazing family especially, my two awesome kids, Jada and Skyler. You two inspire me to be better everyday. I am blessed that God chose me to be your dad. I want to thank my mom for always believing in me as a dreamer that does, rather than simply a dreamer. My sister Abby and my brother-in-law Jon, so thankful for always supporting me and for being great parents to my two nephews, Carson and Neyland. I want to thank my extended family: grandparents, cousins, aunts and uncles. Blessed to have an incredible family, I don't take that for granted. To all of my friends, who always treat me better than I deserve. To all of the pastors and churches that I have worked with over the last 20 plus years. To our current TMM partner churches across the country and the ones that are yet to come. I want to say a special thanks to our friend Keri O for helping us tremendously with her editing skills. Last but certainly not least, my partner in crime (no crimes have been committed, that we know of) Chris Hughes, the true definition of "Framily" (friends who become family.) This is such a fun ride, glad that we get to experience this together. We will have stories for years to come. #JustGettingStarted

Chris's Acknowledgements

I am a blessed man. I've had so many people make an impact on my life. My life is a living testimony to the power of investing in others. I am also so thankful for the many people that have come through my ministry over the last 20+ years. What a blessing to see them all serving and making a difference. I want to say thanks to Avery and Mary Hannah. Avery, you are an amazing young man and God is going to do great things in your life. Mary Hannah, you are such a talented young woman and I know that God is going to use your skills for big things. I'm proud of you all and I love you. Big thanks to my friend Kevin for being there for me through thick and thin over the last 20+ years. You've been like a father/older brother to me. Thanks for just being there. To Jeremy, thanks for being such an amazing friend. You're always a constant and unwavering support and it means the world to get to do this stuff with you. We really are #JustGettingStarted!

Endorsements

Jeremy and Chris cover a lot of "ground" in one book. It's ground every church leader must plow, seed and cultivate if they hope to harvest. This book is a practical and helpful tool to produce more fruit with our labor - and written in a way that God gets all the glory.

Ron Edmondson
CEO - Leadership Network

I love books that make me a better Pastor and leader. *Ministry Mechanics* is practical, biblical and immediately applicable into your ministry. The chapter on finding God's dream for your ministry, is worth the price of the book. Each chapter takes you through a progression of steps that will lead you into God's best for your ministry. You will find tools for your walk with Christ and how to love the church you lead.

Tony Walliser
Lead Pastor
Silverdale Baptist Church - Chattanooga, TN

In The Ministry Mechanics - Build the Church, Equip the Leader, Chris and Jeremy use their experience and lasting friendship to help church leaders achieve more and stay healthy while doing it. This is a great book for any leader at every level of the organization!

Chris Surratt
Author, Ministry Coach

I am so excited about Chris and Jeremy's new book The Ministry Mechanics. These guys not only understand leadership, they understand people. In each chapter you will recognize you're getting insights from real church practitioners, not church growth theorists. Read it with a pen and paper in hand because you will get some good practical steps to help grow a healthy ministry.

Mac Lake
Author, Founder
Developing Leaders with Mac Lake

Rarely is a book a resume for a job. This one is. You will meet two men who believe that the church needs a fresh approach, prompted by fresh eyes. And they are right. When the bread grows stale and moldy, time for a fresh loaf. Read this, and then have a conversation with these guys.

Dan L. Boone
President
Trevecca Nazarene University

Chris and Jeremy invite us to a front row seat with vulnerability and honesty. Sharing critical advice so that we can avoid future pitfalls and lead a healthy, growing church.

Matthew Nickels
Lead Pastor
SilverCreek.church

I love optimistic leaders who have been through the fire! They inspire us to believe anything is possible. Experience like theirs reveals the 'ministry gold' that is only developed in the 'fiery furnace' from a lifetime of faithful service. Simply put, Jeremy and Chris are gold-standard leaders! The wealth of practical ministry best practices in The Ministry Mechanics - Build the Church, Equip the Leader will equip you to create a ministry that not only has immediate impact but also leaves a lasting legacy. Their collaborative efforts flows from passion to see the church revived and the culture engaged. I highly recommend this practical leadership masterpiece!

Dale Sellers
Executive Director
95Network

The reality is that erosion and an unhealthy status quo is the norm for too many churches across the country. Ministry is hard work, and made even harder if you're not equipped with the right tools. What Chris and Jeremy have poured into this book can be the tipping point you need for incredible things to happen not only at your church, but transformation at the personal level as well. I've had the great honor of working with many generals, admirals, CEOs, and leaders of academic institutions and faith-based organizations. Chris is in the top 1% of that group for his leadership, ability to bring people together, and getting things done. Whether your church is thriving or struggling, this impactful book should be considered required reading.

Commander Christopher Cruz
Director, Virtual Education Capabilities
Navy Voluntary Education

Books about building a church, or church leadership, tend to fall in to one of two categories - church *'theory'*, or church *'reality'*. In this book, Chris and Jeremy strike the right balance between helping you dream of what *'could be'* while living and working in the reality of what *'is'*. It's the kind of book that could only come from people who have actually been in the 'trenches' of church ministry. For the Ministry Mechanics, 'Build the Church, Equip the Leader' is more than a catchy tagline for a book, it's a mission!"

Brad Brinkley
Lead Pastor
Unstoppable Church

Jeremy and Chris are able to bring a fresh set of eyes to the ministries of your church. They are able to give you creative and practical solutions that will help your church be productive. Their knowledge of what it takes to help churches grow will be beneficial to any size church. They have been a tremendous help to many churches on the Alabama North District.

Greg Story
District Superintendent
Alabama North District Church of the Nazarene

Chris and Jeremy wear their passion on their sleeves – I have seen it in action, and I have seen church leaders empowered to care for their communities through the clarity that Ministry Mechanics brings to their ministry. When they say the love the church, they mean it. They run alongside leaders with joy, not from a place of having it all figured out, but a place of partnership and support. Their joy is contagious. Building the church is not about a program or steps to success or kit that gets dusty on your shelf. It's about supporting the leader from the inside out, refreshing that calling and restoring the gifts that have been clouded with unnecessary complexity. The answer is clearer than it seems – and I'm thankful that Chris and Jeremy are in my corner.

Mike Lenda
CEO
The Well Coffeehouse

This book flows directly from Chris and Jeremy's deep love for the Church, and it's obvious. Coming from a place of honesty and openness, Chris and Jeremy offer a refreshing reminder to be willing and excited to do whatever it takes to reach people with the message of Christ. And in this book, they'll give you the tools to do exactly that.

Austin Savage
Director of Communications
95Network

As I dig into *"The Ministry Mechanics-Build the Church, Equip the Leader"*, I'm reminded of the importance of keeping the main thing, the main thing, and not only the value, but the necessity of not doing ministry alone. Jeremy and Chris' passion for ministry and partnering with churches, pastors, and leaders jumps off the page as they share the journey and wisdom God has blessed them with. I've been privileged to call Chris a friend, mentor, and ministry partner for several years and have seen in action the principles outlined chapter after chapter. What a blessing to the church at large to have clear, tangible, convicting, and relevant tools to advance God's Kingdom.

James Chavez
Executive Pastor Of MultiSite
Centerpoint Church

www.ingramcontent.com/pod-product-compliance
Lightning Source LLC
Chambersburg PA
CBHW061145040426
42445CB00013B/1554